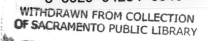

Gardening
BY HEART

Gardening
BY HEART

❧

THE EXTRAORDINARY GIFT

OF AN

ORDINARY GARDEN

Joyce McGreevy

Sierra Club Books
San Francisco

www.sierraclub.org/books

Published by Sierra Club Books, in conjunction with Random House, Inc.

Maude Meehan has generously granted permission to reprint poetry from *Washing the Stones: The Collected Poetry of Maude Meehan*, published in 1996 by Papier Mache Press.

Library of Congress Cataloging-in-Publication Data

McGreevy, Joyce.
    Gardening by heart: the extraordinary gift of an ordinary garden/
        by Joyce McGreevy.
            p.   cm.
    Includes bibliographical references
    ISBN 1-57805-051-0 (alk. paper)
    1. Gardening.   2. McGreevy, Joyce.   I. Title.

SB455 M42   2000   635—dc21   99-049546

Book design by Donna Sinisgalli

In memory
of those whose love, encouragement,
and joy nurtured tender seedlings:
Eddie Kwock, Regina Hicks, Dorothy Chelew,
Mary and Gerald Palfrey,
and my parents, Helen Collins McGreevy and Wallace McGreevy

In celebration
of all my family and friends,
whose presence in my life can make the most
ordinary day into a garden of sweet surprises:
Love to each of you, dear ones

In gratitude
to my teachers, especially
Amber Jayanti and Hubert McDermott,
and to a fellow gardener of word, earth, and heart,
my editor, Linda Gunnarson

CONTENTS

Autumn

HONORING THE HARVEST

Winter

TRUSTING THE FROST

ACKNOWLEDGMENTS

In my heart I send: a bucket of organic daisies to Jerry, with love; Mom's Lincoln roses to Michael McGreevy, especially for the night he pointed a projector out an apartment window in Ventura to give us a slide show on a brick wall, and we talked about projecting our visions beyond our circumstances; a glorious mixed bouquet to my brothers and sisters for a shared wealth of stories; seeds of future gardens to Eoghan, Allison, Shawn, Fontaine, Maggie, Ethan, Rory, Ariele, Talleri, Antonia, Ashley, Rebecca, Cian, Aelia, Benen, and all my nieces and nephews; exotic orchids to Cindy Fee, whose soulful singing, cooking, and creative fire I depend upon; sweet peas in a vase designed by Lynne Willis for her, Kat, Janee, Jani, Anya, Mimi, and all in the Bloomers Creativity Circle; lavender to Sheryl and Paul Finnegan for sharing their calm when mine was missing; Ojai blossoms to Linda and Joe Hancock, Eleanor and Ray Harder and George Woods for making a big production out of things; a Poet's Corner for Maude Meehan, Maggie Paul, Daphne Crocker-White, and Tony

White for poems that inspire; Van Gogh sunflowers to Katherine Johnson for affirmation and wicked wit; wild ginger for Rick Chelew, who helped out in a hundred ways; a perfect rose to Julie Cason for showing me the power of pruning; a gourmet salad with edible flowers to Harvey Landa and Kateri McRae for stepping in when I needed to step out; a lotus blossom each to Joyce Sherry and Pamela Shipley for reminding me what matters; heart's ease to Bernice Kwock McGreevy who offered just that, even when she needed it herself; wild irises to Bernard Pregerson and Amber Jayanti for clear sight and beautiful ways; bells of Ireland to Joan Sheehy and Barbara Collins for never forgetting; picture-perfect dahlias to Dan and Sally Welsh-Bon for keeping me in focus; wild mountain heather to the Staffords of Ireland and Australia for turning what could have been rocky soil into fragrant gardens; *fiori della Toscana* for Carl Alasko, Elizabeth Dawkins, Nat and Leslie Klein for *gentilezza;* enough begonias to fill a diva's dressing room to David Lansford and Mary Haas for saving me from serious error; a host of yellow daffodils to Joan Ackerman for teaching me to learn; no-fuss nasturtiums to the staff of Sierra Club Books and Random House, as well as to freelance copyeditor Janet Baker who took great care every step of the way; a basket of California lupines to my agent, Barb Doyen, for believing in the manuscript.

All that we did, all that we said or sang

Must come from contact with the soil. . . .

— William Butler Yeats,
"The Municipal Gallery Revisited"

INTRODUCTION

This is a story of how the seeds of grief flowered into a harvest of joy. It begins in an ordinary garden and spreads, like sweet alyssum, into gardens beyond. It ends in the realization that every flowerpot and poppy field, every urban terrace and backyard vegetable patch, every chaparral-covered mountain, and every sidewalk cracked open by a daisy is a part of that remarkable garden we call the earth.

People who come to my garden say that it gives them a

✿

deep sense of happiness to be there. I think it has to do less with design, choice of plants, or my individual skills than with the way I am learning to simply listen, however imperfectly, for the voice of nature. I hear it in each and every aspect of gardening I undertake. Nature continually tells us what it needs, and we, being a part of nature, may safely bring our own longings into the light and nurture of the garden.

Although it is not intended as a step-by-step manual, *Gardening by Heart* offers itself as a creative reference to garden lovers at all levels of experience. In the essays that follow you will find a potpourri of quotations, recipes, and resources for further reading. Here, too, is a bushel of practical, creative, and occasionally preposterous ideas. Along with tips about discouraging snails, sharing the garden's abundance, and fostering a love of gardening in young people, you will also come across suggestions for keeping a nature journal at the office, choosing the appropriate weeds for dinner, and making the most of knowing nothing.

Part memoir, part garden philosophy, this book is a call not only to tend your home garden but to consider gardens at the workplace, in schools, and elsewhere in the community. Above all, I encourage you to lavish care on the garden of your heart. If all this sunlight and soil, wind and rain have any meaning at all, surely it is found there. Thus sorrow is composted into possibility, and happiness runs riot where once there was only the barrenness of pain. As Henry David Thoreau wrote in *Walden*, "If the day and the night are such that you greet them with joy, and life emits a fragrance like flowers and sweet-scented herbs . . . that is your success."

In welcoming you to *Gardening by Heart,* I lead you into the Garden of Memory, past the glossy Garden of Hype, and on to the Imperfect Garden of Infinite Possibility. In so doing, I invite you to enter, as if for the first time, into that garden you call your own. Whether it consists of several acres in the country or a single window box in an urban apartment, therein lie all the mysteries of life. An extravagant claim? Touch the soil, releasing its scent into the air. Plant and nurture a single seed. Attend it daily. What blossoms before you will be a miracle. What blossoms within you may astonish you.

Gardening
BY HEART

Spring

WATERING

THE

SEED

The land is a mother that never dies.

—Maori wisdom

GRIEF IS A SEED

In classical mythology, the birth of a new crop sometimes begins with the death of the Corn Maiden. My garden began with the death of my mother.

Cancer informed, but could not dictate, the last five years of Mom's life. Once, when a nurse suggested that she cultivate an appreciation for life's singular moments, Mom was flooded with joy—for she realized she had always done just that. Indeed, *cultivate* was the operative word.

A gifted artist and avid reader, Helen Collins McGreevy was also an inspired gardener, and it was in the garden that she frequently discovered, and drew her family's attention to, emblems of ordinary magic. The way a California sunset emboldened the glow of red flowers, making them bob like lanterns in a river of green shadow. The sweet crunch of summer's first corn. The comical sight of twin bullfrogs promenading along the terraced walkway.

Citing Eastern religion, Mom used to say that when we died the success or failure of our lives would come down to two questions: Did you find joy? Did you bring joy? Those questions apply equally well to my mother's way of gardening. For hers was a lifelong process of self-fulfillment and generosity.

My mother's garden was filled with hidden delights. Tucked like Easter eggs among pansies, marigolds, and other edible flowers were strawberries for grandchildren to find. A sitting area dubbed the Poets' Corner, enclosed within natural walls of climbing roses and hibiscus, became a favorite hideout, a place where, as our father put it, you could sit and "just be"—no small achievement when you are the parents of eight children.

The fruits and vegetables my siblings carried to Mom by the armloads became dinners to savor and paintings to treasure. The scent of home-picked lemons, we have discovered, rubs off not only on one's skin but also on one's memory.

❦

I had never been much of a gardener. I was more of a garden spectator. Confident as a hummingbird at a well-maintained feeder, I looked to Mom's garden to nourish my senses, then buzzed off to a more interior life.

In Ireland, where I went to college and married my first husband, I did little gardening. The world was just naturally green. Tilling stony soil could not compete with the rigors and joys of studying at the university in Galway, publishing poetry, going into features writing, and reviewing new scripts for the Druid and Abbey Theatres.

When I returned to California to take up a position as editor for an educational publishing company, I was a single mother with little time left over to care for myself, let alone a plant. Yet throughout those years, I was drawn to the idea of a garden in general and to memories of my mother's garden in particular.

Now and then I would start a garden, with no clue as to what grew well where, enjoying a fortnight of ill-tended verdure before the brown reality set in. Invariably, I concluded that I was just not a gardener and had best leave the mysterious art to its natural-born initiates.

❧

Mom died during one of the most lavish springs that drought-stricken California had experienced in several years. Rain lashed the earth and set off a torrent of purple lupine, gold poppies, and other wildflowers. Stubbly manila-colored hills became ocean swells of green sage and wild oats. The beauty angered me. In the face of death, the continuum of nature seemed obscene.

GARDENING
BY HEART

> *This spring the colours pierce,*
> *too opulent, too vivid. . . .*
>
> *Something bruised in me*
> *longs for gardens of my childhood.*
>
> —MAUDE MEEHAN, "SECOND SPRING"

Meanwhile, I had married Jerry Sinclair, moving into the whimsical, old-fashioned house that he built in the sage- and oak-covered hills of northern Monterey County. I had also left the publishing company, where overtime was as routine as unscheduled weekends were rare. I opted instead to work freelance and spend more time—as in *any* time—with my family. A seasoned workaholic, I was a type A who had paused but not relented some years back when an upset stomach turned out to be a rare disorder requiring emergency surgery. Now, contemplating the entirely new life before me, I had a sudden dismal preview of how I might end up approaching it.

There I'd sit, cooped up inside the house attempting to "cure" my grief by being the best darned little freelancer that ever drew the blinds and stared at the computer screen.

Then I rejected the image.

It was Mom's brother Ray, a retired biology teacher and gardening adept, who suggested that each family member take a cutting from Mom's garden and transplant it into his or her own. The symbolism of the ritual was not lost on us. With Mom's death, following hard upon a series of strokes that eventually took our father from us, plus the sale of the family home we had loved and revisited for more than thirty years, we were as raw and uncertain as cuttings hacked from a parent plant.

How to take root in this strange new soil fenced off by grief? None of us knew. But nature did, and thus the idea of a garden was born. Grief was the seed.

"What kind of a cutting would you like?" Ray asked. I pointed to a blue spiny herb, the scent of which has, even now, the power to conjure up my mother's kitchen in vivid detail, right down to the feel of the Irish linen tablecloth and the companionable music of my parents' conversation.

It was rosemary, I knew that much. What I didn't know then is that each of the world's numerous herbs possesses a distinctive history, a legacy of its healing properties, mythic lore, and perceptual associations. Traditionally, rosemary has been used to heal despondency. It is associated with Mary the mother of Jesus and other archetypes of the Mother.

And rosemary is the herb of remembrance.

The lessons of the garden had begun.

Gardens were before gardeners, and but some hours after the earth.

—*Sir Thomas Browne,*
The Garden of Cyrus

WHAT IS A GARDEN?

When you picture a garden, what comes to mind? Rolling acres of manicured lawn and formal topiary? A painter's palette of blooms untouched by weeds, bugs, or seasonal droop?

Or do you see a few bachelor buttons poking their blue heads above the backyard's wild grass? A small but promising native pine where once there was only the bare ground of a housing development? Three pots of cheery pepperomia on a windowsill?

Too often, our image of what's acceptable as a bare minimum is based on the grandest scenario imaginable. Glossy gardening magazines and catalogs don't help. Many a novice gardener has thrown in the trowel after "failing" to produce the lush and weedless copy of a retouched photo spread.

Am I suggesting that you limit your dream garden? Not at all. If you want to grow sunflowers in the snow or re-create the Boboli Gardens on your balcony, go ahead. But don't let the garden of your dreams close the gate on the garden that you have.

I once knew a man who said he longed to learn piano. So why didn't he? I asked. Because, he explained, the only thing he wanted to play was Gershwin's "Rhapsody in Blue," a work many virtuosos might consider a challenge. What about the basics? I asked. Even Gershwin must have put in his share of five-finger exercises. "No way," my friend responded seriously. "I don't want to fool around. It's 'Rhapsody in Blue' or nothing." So he chose nothing. His very goal kept him both from achieving the goal and from experiencing smaller joys along the way—hearing two notes merge into a chord, playing a melody line by heart.

We risk stunting our own growth as gardeners when we intimidate ourselves with extravagant notions of what a garden "should" be. So let's take a closer look at some of those glossy gardens. They aren't what they seem.

Take the magazine cover depicting a certain celebrity out

"working" in her garden. Clad in a pearl-gray skirt and a white silk blouse with billowing sleeves, she is holding a delicate seedling and a small ceramic pot in her immaculately groomed hands. In the background, a lavish rose garden attests to her apparent ability to maintain a floral paradise without breaking her long nails, tripping on her hem, or tearing the heck out of those sheer and copious sleeves.

Then there's the photo essay about the family in the American Southwest whose garden looks like something straight out of *Brideshead Revisited*. There's not a cactus, a cottonwood, or a hint of that quintessentially southwestern red soil in sight. Nothing, in fact, to locate the viewer in that unique and magnificent bioregion—a region where the rainfall is considerably lower than the water level required to maintain such fussy blooms.

Perhaps the worst insults to a gardener's intelligence are those articles in which a single gardener—again, dressed more for a state dinner or high tea than for scrabbling around in the gooseweed—is credited with the work of achieving a garden on par with the grounds at Versailles. Tucked discreetly into a caption or at the end of the commentary will be a cursory reference to the professional gardeners and crew who "provided encouragement." One pictures this anonymous team cheering on Mr. or Mrs. Mulchwell from behind the shrubbery.

The simple truth is this: A garden is whatever you can raise. It is that place of conscious relationship with nature in which one becomes apprentice and steward to what grows.

What grows, ideally, will have less to do with fixed models on the gardener's part than with a gradually honed perceptiveness of the garden's own intentions—with the inherent longing of the land—based on a careful reading of soil, microclimate, size, direction of sunlight, history, and other clues.

The word *garden* comes from the Old English verb *gardyn*, meaning "to enclose." On one hand, then, we derive the stereotype of the garden as one's own private Eden, a site of order and beauty, closed off from the chaos and brutalities of the outside world.

Yet there is another way to look at it. When you bring daily attention to what blossoms, dies, and returns to the earth, you soon discover that the smallest aspect of the garden holds within it the vast store of nature's wisdom. Seen from this perspective, the cosmos flower is well named, because like any organism it encloses the greater cosmos, right down to the planetlike electrons that orbit the brilliant suns of its nuclei.

At the same time, intimate involvement with a particular garden increases one's own sense of belonging to nature, of being lovingly enclosed within the unlimited mystery.

By extension, even such an enclosure as the margin of dirt between an apartment block and a sidewalk can, by gardening, be brought back into nature's continuum. I know of a woman who turned just such an unpromising ribbon of soil into a dazzling forest of sunflowers, each one of which was the joy and responsibility of the young people who lived in her apartment complex. Passersby stopped to admire the flowers. Birds came for the seeds. Butterflies were seen for the first summer that anyone could remember. And within the hearts of the younger tenants, the seeds of nature were given room to grow.

Even on the busiest days, I pass through gardens of extraordinary beauty and in unlikely places. Here in our little town there is a doughnut shop. A few years ago, this shop underwent a change in owners and its business soared. How to explain it? After all, the old owners were pleasant enough and, no, the cost of doughnuts wasn't slashed. Indeed, the new owner makes the same old doughnuts in the same old way, and the simple furnishings are set up just as before. But the woman who owns the bakery radiates so much joy that it draws people in like a magnet. I have watched as the grouchiest, grizzled old truck drivers shamble in there, only to emerge wearing smiles they probably haven't used since they were nine years old.

What does all this have to do with gardening, you ask? Well, it's a curious thing, but recently the owner began filling her shop with cuttings of indoor greenery. Nothing special, just the usual assortment of philodendrons, pepperomia, and so forth. Now you have to understand that the bakery, which is lit by the ubiquitous fluorescent overheads, has only two small windows in the front, and those are shaded by an overhanging arch, hardly an ideal setup for growing anything. Yet within weeks, those plants had, without benefit of chemicals, burgeoned into lush and massive manifestations of the life force. I'm convinced that they, like everyone else, responded to the owner's joy. Not surprisingly, the name of her place is The Sunshine Bakery.

Such, then, is a garden, a place where life bubbles forth like innocent laughter and where the sense of place reflects the essence of the gardener. The foyer of my poet friend Maude Meehan's house is a case in point. Ignoring gardening manuals that dictate which plants go with which, Maude has filled her mini-greenhouse with plants in precisely the manner that she has filled her heart with friends. They may be fussy or self-sufficient, extravagant or timid, so long as they have roots in the earth and a tendency toward the light. The crowning glory of this eclectic garden is a pair of elegant dracaenas. Set side by side, their regal, tapering stems began to entwine following the death of Maude's beloved husband. Sweethearts since Maude was fourteen, they had been married for fifty-seven years. Of course, one could argue that the plants just happened to entwine, but standing there in that bower of wild harmony, one feels the embrace of a greater truth.

Come into the garden, Maud,
For the black bat, night, has flown,
Come into the garden, Maud,
I am here at the gate alone;
And the woodbine spices are wafted abroad,
And the musk of the roses blown.

—ALFRED, LORD TENNYSON, "MAUD"

If a journey begins with a single step, then a garden begins with a single seed. That seed may be a spider plant bringing the energy of nature into an office; a mindfully dug patch of soil ready to receive the first segments of potato; petunias in a south-facing window box, taking the noontime blaze with easy grace; a sweet-pea seed forming itself into the vibrant surprise that will turn a battered trash can and gray fence into elements of beauty's composition. One of the most stunning gardens that ever caused me to catch my breath contained only a single tree. November had turned its leaves to a yellow as potent and dazzling as sudden sunlight in a cloudy sky. Leaves shimmered in the branches and piled in great golden snowdrifts across the lawn.

Whatever grows, evolves. A pot of mint today may lead eventually to that Shakespearean herb garden sought out by horticultural tourists. Yet in one sense there is no ideal garden for the gardener, only the process of gardening itself. Just as Picasso experimented with new ideas even toward the end of his life, a gardener may follow an impulse toward the rare and exotic. Just as a Zen practitioner may clear away decades' worth of learning in order to return to the beginner's mind, a gardener may spend whole seasons observing the daily progress of a tomato plant.

Meanwhile, our lives are filled with gardens if only we would take the time to look.

For years, I managed to live in California without a car. Every day I would walk with my son through a park, a town, and the beginnings of a forest to his school, then turn back and head east to the office. The hedgerows and ditches soon became our equivalent of Edith Holden's *Country Diary of an Edwardian Lady.* The progress of wildflowers conferred a blessing on each and every weekday. Spring announced itself in the pungent aroma of sage. Even in winter, sparrows and starlings made it clear that thick brown brambles could be a haven.

Now, like most adults, I drive. But walking remains an essential part of the day. With the increasing number of cars and the ever-widening highways, it's been all too easy for nature to get blurred and cordoned off, its very existence threatened. In such a speed-driven culture, gardens themselves may become little more than décor, something to mark the perimeters of a shopping mall or fill in a property quickly to increase its market value. To spend time sitting in a garden, or to take a walk and look at the gardens in one's area, becomes an unthinkable luxury. Instead, we flip through magazines at the doctor's office, glance at scenes of pastoral grandiosity, and decide, "I could never achieve *that.*"

But gardens are all around us. They include the flower that pokes up through an urban sidewalk. The massive tree kids love to climb that someone's great-great-great-grandparent set into the ground as a sapling. A cool grotto in, of all places, the courtyard of your dentist. The stand of "weeds" in your backyard that turns out to be mostly native herbs. A stubble of green moss on a concrete wall after the first spring rains. The bountiful outpouring of geraniums filling the balcony of a studio apartment. A whiff of orange blossom as you pass the post office.

This week, instead of just going about your usual routine, take a little time to notice whatever grows in your area. Harvest those secret gardens—from the daisy in the parking lot to the almond blossoms along the highway—by making a home for them in your senses. Who knows what seeds of inspiration might spring from the earth of your expanded awareness?

WHAT IS A
GARDEN?

My garden will never make me famous,
I'm a horticultural ignoramus.

—*Ogden Nash,*
"He Digs, He Dug, He Has Dug"

GARDENING
WITHOUT A CLUE

Recently, a friend in Monterey noticed a garden on her street that appeared to be the only one not ravaged by gophers. An experienced gardener herself, she still had occasional problems with the voracious rodents. Deciding to investigate, she walked over and said hello to her neighbor. Midway into their conversation she mentioned the gophers or, rather, the lack of them. "What's your secret?" she asked, hoping it didn't involve a shotgun or one of those gruesome medieval traps with spikes.

"Oh, it's no secret," he replied. "As soon as I see a hole I take some tongs and set a piece of rotting squid into it."

"Rotting . . . squid?" my friend murmured.

"That's right. Rotting squid. They hate the smell, so they stay away. Haven't had gophers here for years. And I'll tell you something else. My roses thrive on that squid. Can't get enough."

True enough, the man's rosebushes were heavy with blooms, whose perfume, and mercifully not that of the squid, permeated the air.

Since that day, my friend has been experimenting with a variety of fish in those parts of her garden not already proofed with gopher wire. The local fish market is only too happy to give the old stuff away. The results have been remarkable.

More importantly, she has stayed in touch with her fellow gardener. She figures that this retired commercial fisherman must know his fish. And that a gardener of his age—he's close to one hundred—has probably learned a thing or two about other matters. Now *that's* experience.

You are probably familiar with the Zen saying, "When the student is ready, the teacher will come." I've seen it borne out time and time again, and it's certainly true with gardening.

I started off gardening without a clue. Yet after a time, even that becomes a teacher. None of the many books I read told me that the eggplants and peppers I'd set in a bed near the tomato starts would end up shaded by them. Yes, common sense might have spoken up, but my common sense tends to operate on a noninterventionist policy. In the end, it was nature who showed me why my initially burgeoning plants set puny little specimens with a habit of self-destructing. I'd simply planted those vegetables on the wrong side. That one failure taught me volumes about the importance of positioning in the garden.

I've made other errors, too, and learned from every one. Watching the first broccoli plant that I had grown from seed disappear before my very eyes within moments, as if drowning in quicksand, goaded me to find out about gopher wire. It also woke up my respect for all the preparatory steps that novice gardeners tend to skip over.

My dad used to joke that life is too short to learn by experience. In large measure, he was right. Not every trial and error are survivable. But in the garden, experience is the wisest teacher of all. If the wealth of information in books and other gardeners is to be fully appreciated, you need to become as familiar with your garden as with a growing child. That takes time and attention—your time, your attention. No book, no matter how informative, can provide you with the vital particulars of that relationship. You learn it by living it.

Once I visited Tuolumne Meadows in Yosemite National Park with a group of writers. Like everyone else, I expected that our brilliant teachers Inka Christiansen and Paul Tidwell would pack us full of information. I can still picture the ten of us following like ducklings, notebooks at the ready, poised to jot down this term, that statistic.

Instead, they directed us to study the land in silence and to write down as many questions as we could come up with. Those questions, which reflected a wide range of backgrounds, sensory awareness, and longing, provided our group with a framework as durable and complex as the web of a Yosemite spider. More importantly, the act of silent questioning called for each of us to enter into the place rather than stand apart from it. "Where does nature begin?" Paul had asked us, in order to start off the questioning. Soon we realized that we were looking not *at* but *from* the very heart of nature.

I have since brought that valuable ritual into other areas of my life, the garden included. If it's true, as Einstein contended, that imagination is more important than knowledge, gardeners are clearly not loafing whenever they wander the grounds or sit and gaze at the flowers. Why else are we here if not to notice and to love what is around us?

One of the most powerful lessons I learned in paying attention came from a teacher who was all of nineteen months old. Smaller than your average garden gnome, Anouk looked like France's solemn answer to Shirley Temple. As I followed her around the garden of my brother Michael and his wife, Bernice, I realized that Anouk not only looked at the garden, she listened to and felt it as well. She liked the feel of pillowy, cool chrysanthemums and grasses brushing against her little legs. The sound of a bee going about its work delighted her.

Following the sound with her, I sank to my knees and brought my eyes level with Anouk's line of vision. Only then was I able to detect the mixed scent of damp soil and sun-warmed grass. We stared into a pocket-size cave of shrubbery, where a white peony gleamed like a lantern, and watched the bee climb deep into its center and emerge with its back legs fat with bright yellow pollen.

It had been a long time, I realized afterward, since I had simply explored and experienced a garden.

Now I take the lesson of Anouk with me, bringing all the senses out into the garden as purposefully as one would tote an assortment of rakes, shovels, and trowels. I listen for wind rustling the corn and the starflowers, the curious grinding music of the hummingbirds, the *pock-pock* of sunflower seeds falling to the ground and setting off the skitter of a dusty blue lizard into the cool of the artemisia. I pause to inhale the fragrance of lavender or to pop a sky-blue borage flower into my mouth, savoring its delicate texture and cucumber taste. Here and there I put my palms to the soil to test for dryness or scoop with my fingers to make sure that beneficial earthworms are still in residence.

I bring a sense of wonder, too, mentally compiling questions for further study even as my heart encounters questions for which there are no answers, but only a deepening sense of the mystery. Harvesting questions is an essential component of the gardener's work.

Gardening books became more accessible once I had gathered a few seasons' worth of questions. From not knowing where to start in a voluminous text, or how to retain all the information, I now had specific concerns and a personal schema on which to organize ideas.

The same experiential approach helped enormously when I paid a mere $13 and signed up for a semester's worth of organic gardening classes at Monterey Peninsula College. Most of us students had been mucking about the best we could for some years, and the collective wealth of fool's luck, serendipity, baffling situations, bitter failures, and sudden insights proved as useful as Sandra Forman's excellent demonstrations and assigned texts.

For instance, the section on minerals and organic soil amendment really hit home when one embarrassed student described the results of soaking peas with a commercial fertilizer highly touted as a wonder product. Because she was steeping in nitrogen a plant that was already a magnet for naturally occurring nitrogen, the plant tripled in size, turned an eye-popping intensity of green—and produced almost no peas at all.

That experience prompted another student to remind us of something he had learned while traveling in the Southwest. While listening to a storyteller give an account of how Bean Woman had fallen in love with Corn Man, he found out that for thousands of years Native American growers have wisely planted corn and beans together. The cornstalks support the twining tendrils of the beans, and the soil-enriching beans re-place the minerals removed by the heavy-feeding corn.

Meanwhile, Sandra would often amend what the books had to say about intensive gardening. After all, for several years she had lived in France, the very place where intensive gardening was born.

Again and again, even as we studied the facts, our experiences, questions, and problems combined to produce the richest yield of ideas. While brainstorming organic methods of dealing with snails, one student recalled that his grandmother in Wales, who raised chickens, had successfully protected new plants by ringing them with crushed eggshells. Another student reported similar results with cold wood ash. One recalled that ordinary bran seemed to do the trick. Someone else had recycled their tired spices in such a way. Another mixed up wormwood and horseradish in a spray solution. One made collars from sandpaper, while still another routinely invited neighborhood kids to participate in a snail-picking contest, with prizes for the ones who found the most.

Numerous other alternatives to bait and beer-trap methods were debated. It struck me that while occasionally pooling the benefits of what we had read, we were more frequently pooling what we had experienced.

This is not to suggest that you discount the wealth of information available in books. I'm too much the bibliophile to utter such heresy as that. However, just as a garden needs good soil, the fruit of great books grows best when the medium of your own experience is rich enough to support it.

Nowhere is this better illustrated than when it comes to tomato growing. Depending on which books you read, tomatoes should be watered infrequently, often, or never. They must be fertilized. They don't need to be fertilized. The compost should or should not include shredded tomato plants. It's imperative that you prune them. No, leave them alone. Other contradictions abound in gardening, but the point is clear. Sooner or later, you just have to try something and see what happens.

Discoveries get made this way.

For example, when I noticed that certain plants did not appeal to snails, I added more of those to the garden and made a point of observing the plants themselves. Several of the plants had a perfume that may have rendered them too pungent for a snail's palate. Others, I noticed, had rough surfaces inhospitable to delicate bodies. Still others attracted birds that might have added snails to their menu. After a while, even the plants that did attract snails became convenient decoys and made hand-picking less of a chore.

As you can see, I'm still at the *may have, might,* and *maybe* stage. That's okay. Every square foot of my garden, both cultivated and wild, is a study-in-progress, and everywhere I look I see teachers. Both that first crop of leggy collapsing radishes and the sight of deep green oaks on a sunburnt hill taught me the importance of seed depth to the formation of strong, healthy roots and stems. The taste of sweet strawberries brings back the memory of my mother, who showed me how to feed oak leaves into the soil of these acid-loving plants. The sound of a hummingbird hovering boldly within hand-brushing distance of my face reminds me to deadhead the spent flowers to speed fresh nectar-producing blooms.

If I could map these years of study, it would show the winding path of a Parsifal, that knight who found the Holy Grail not despite but precisely because of his habit of stumbling along, forging foolishly into unknown territory, trusting this, trying that, and asking "dumb" questions. If the Grail itself eludes me, there are still successes fertilized by setbacks—areas where a wise elder (human, animal, or vegetable) offered assistance—and a host of happy surprises. Perhaps that *is* the Grail, the ever-filling cup of one's life experience, in which case the path leads not away but always deeper into the here and now.

Even the literal pathways in my garden reflect a process of wandering realization. Their design did not precede the flower garden but evolved over several growing cycles, as my family discovered where we and the various other animals tended to walk, which plants flowed like rivers, mounded like hills, or climbed skyward, and how one area tended to island itself from the next. The eventual pathways that Jerry and I laid rambled and curved in far more creative and natural ways than anything we could have designed on graph paper or a computer screen.

There is, of course, one very effective method of avoiding all guesswork in the garden: Let someone else do it. Recently I visited a gentleman whose elegant garden is entirely maintained by professionals. When I mentioned that the anemones were looking particularly beautiful, he replied, "What are those?" I pointed them out. "Oh, right," he said. "I'm so used to them, *I don't really notice anymore*." How sad to live amid beauty and not to see it, to "own" it and not to experience it. Had he personally amended the soil, planted the bulbs, and tended the plants that broke through the earth, I guarantee he would have noticed. Without that degree of involvement, he was missing out on the very thing itself.

The seed of the garden is the heart of the gardener, stirred into conscious connection with the land. As such, the goal of a garden becomes not an end product but an ongoing relationship, not a testament to one's control, status, or expertise but a place of constant wonder.

The fruit of the garden is gardening. The fruit of gardening is the blossoming of new eyes.

*T*hen a sentimental passion of a vegetable fashion
must excite your languid spleen,
An attachment à la Plato for a bashful young potato
or a not too French French bean!

—W. S. Gilbert, Patience, *Act I*

THE POTATO QUEEN

Every gardener has one special plant, one horticultural high
achiever that makes up for all the stragglers, fussbudgets, and
failures. It may be an heirloom rose, a rare orchid, or a prize-
winning apple.

For me, it's the potato.

I've been called a lot of things in my life, but my preferred
title is "The Potato Queen."

I never know from summer to summer whether the tomatoes will thrive or die. When I broadcast wildflower seeds, it's always a contest to see whether the rain or the scrub jays will get to them first. But twelve weeks after I put those dear little seed potatoes to bed, I know for certain that tiny flowers of white, gold, or purple will pop from the top of each leafy stalk. You can have your crocuses and your roses. To my mind, the most beautiful flower in the world is the potato flower, a true harbinger of good news: namely, the arrival of buried treasure.

Now many a fruit or vegetable relies upon your patience, as anyone knows who has ever sampled a lemony-sour plum or an eraser-like stalk of celery. But potato plants have an indulgent way with the vagaries of human nature. Oh, go ahead, they say, with all the magnanimity of a fridge to a midnight snacker. Sure enough, if I carefully brush away the soil around the plant I will uncover tubers the size of quail eggs and in colors that range from deep amethyst and ruby to gold and gleaming white. At such a moment, I am seized with rapture and likely to be struck by such giddy insights as *It was for this — this! — that I minored in archaeology!*

Yes, I'll admit it, I'm mad for spuds. As Shakespeare so wisely wrote in *The Merry Wives of Windsor,* "Let the skies rain potatoes."

This passion for the potato is heightened by the fact that if, after sampling a few dinners' worth of new ones, you return to the ground of your delight, you can still harvest enough behemoths to see you through the winter. And when the time comes to rotate your crop, you'll find that the soil in the potato bed, no matter how tough it was to begin with, is now as fine as flour.

It seems curious to me, spud fanatic that I am, that sonneteers have long favored roses over potatoes as a poetic emblem. For starters, potatoes have some of the most evocative names in the language of gardening. Names like Kerr's Pink, Green Mountain, and Viking Purple. Bliss Triumph and Seneca Horn. Kasaan, Katahdin, Kennebec. Ruby Crescent, Garnet Chile, and Yukon Gold. If potatoes lack the convenient irony of thorns, they more than make up for it by offering a mysterious subterranean life suggestive of the rich workings of the subconscious. And while many a maid has been compared, with overarching imprecision, to a rose, doesn't the potato more accurately correspond to your dear one's dimpled knees and irregular if beloved countenance? The way I see it, Robbie Burns might just as passionately have declared:

> *Oh, my luve is like a red, red Norland*
> *That's newly boiled in June.*

Tell me *that* isn't—uh, steamy. Gather ye russets while ye may, that's my motto.

The term *couch potato,* used to describe some lazy soul who "vegetates" in a dark room watching TV, could only have been coined in the United States. Elsewhere, the potato has been seen as a prodigious sustainer of human life.

In the Incan civilization, which was otherwise based on corn, the potato was the only major crop that could thrive at altitudes higher than ten thousand feet. In Ireland, where the first potatoes arrived in the late 1500s—no one knows how— the potato became first a lifesaver and then a symbol of injustice, desperation, and tragedy.

According to Joan Elma Rahn, author of *Plants That Changed History*, at the time of the potato's arrival, "most of the Irish tenanted land that had been taken from them by the invading English. [The potato] proved much easier to grow than the cereal grains to which the Irish had been accustomed." The potato crop flourished in stony ground and promised high yield. Equally important in a land where rain can be a near-constant tide sweeping over the land, the harvest date was not as critical as that of grain.

"In the early 1800s," writes Rahn, "nearly all the land in Ireland was owned by only about eight thousand persons, many of them English and living in England—that is, it was owned by absentee landlords." The farmers paid exorbitant rents for lands that had once belonged to them outright. The rent traveled through a series of middlemen—each one of whom had padded it for his own profit—before reaching the absentee landlord.

I have often heard well-meaning fellow Americans, including many with an Irish surname, attribute the Irish potato famine to the quaint notion that the Irish made the mistake of growing a single crop, which then failed. In fact, the Irish were sophisticated farmers who grew a diversity of grains, including oats, wheat, and barley. The practice of making such an exotic import as the potato their staple food must have required considerable adjustment.

By the 1800s, however, farmers were selling their expensive grain crops just to keep up with the rents. Nothing could be held in reserve, for every last bit of cash crop was needed, and there was rarely much money left over. Others had been pushed off more arable land onto strips of bog. This left farmers with no choice but to subsist on potatoes.

Then, in 1845, nearly half the potato crop of Ireland was destroyed by blight.

It was tragedy on a bizarre scale, for the plentiful supplies of Irish grain continued to be shipped to other countries while the people who produced it literally starved. Famine conditions struck again in 1859 and 1879. During this time, more than a million Irish left the country. Another million and a half died.

One century later, in 1985, a massive famine struck Ethiopia. Ireland, one of the smallest and least populated European countries, was nevertheless among the biggest contributors to the famine relief effort. Memories of the Great Hunger have survived even the passing of generations.

While the history-making potato is one of the most widely traveled vegetables on earth—from the Andes to Ireland is quite a jaunt—it has also boldly gone where no vegetable had gone before. Recently, astronauts became astroculturists when they grew potatoes on the space shuttle Columbia. In its efforts to find ways to grow food for astronauts NASA has, in its own systematic way, become as enamored of spuds as I have. After all, they reason, the potato appeals to just about every palate and is a storehouse of nutrients and slow-burning energy. There's also no waste and it's easy to prepare, important considerations when the chef is floating about in zero gravity.

In my family, as long as there are potatoes in the garden there is dinner for the table, and with no trip to the store. Boil the potatoes gently with their skins on, drizzle them with butter and fresh herbs. Add soup, a salad, or other steamed veggies, anything that doesn't mind being eclipsed by the ecstasy-inducing taste of organic home-grown spuds. We have watched friends, especially those used to eating chain-store clones that come in a single variety (bland), slip into states of bliss so transcendent one might have expected them to leave their car in our driveway and waft home on a cloud.

The point of all this is that somewhere in your gardening repertoire, as in the wider garden of your life, lies the wonder plant whose magic precisely matches your ability to tend it. A friend of mine insists that she is not a gardener because the only things she can grow are petunias. But I guarantee you've never seen petunias until you've seen these petunias. You open the wooden gate into Joan's four-by-ten-foot garden, and wave upon vibrant wave of crimson and violet flowers look up at you like sensuous lips inviting you to an orgy. You could get into a lot of trouble in a garden like that, and you wouldn't be sorry. Just as well, I suppose, that a heavenly host of white petunias trumpets glory and goodness along the margins.

Find what thrives for you and grow it. It may be a staggering collection of sunflower types. The sweetest apricots anyone ever tasted. Or it may, quite literally, amount to a hill of beans.

Ah, but what beans!

One cannot but be in awe when [one] contemplates the mysteries of eternity, of life, of the marvelous structure of reality. It is enough if one tries merely to comprehend a little of this mystery each day. Never lose a holy curiosity.

—*Albert Einstein, quoted in Ronald W. Clark,*
Einstein: The Life and Times

SACRED GARDENS
ARE EVERYWHERE

Imagine a garden dense with flowers, a place apart from the rushing world. The fragrance of lavender rises up like incense, uplifting the heart and quieting the mind. Helichrysum flows like a stream, glinting lime gold in the sun. Along its banks of foliage one finds deep blue pansies, petunias violet as the rainbow's seventh ray, and the scattered sparkle of chrysanthemum daisies. Here and there the glowing yellow lantern of an

Iceland poppy appears like a bird asserting its bright song in a dark wood.

Suddenly, from some invisible point in the sky, a ruby-throated hummingbird descends into the garden, vibrating the air with its fiery blur of wings. It hovers just long enough for the one who has come to the garden heavyhearted to feel, once more, the astonished joy of being alive.

Now consider the dimensions of this place—approximately six feet by six inches.

It is my window box.

True, I cannot stroll within this miniature Eden, but when I throw open the windows, pull up a chair, and lean into its healing atmosphere, it might just as easily be the Temple Gardens of Kyoto. In the middle of many a hectic day I have stopped by for spiritual and aesthetic renewal, reaching out a hand to touch the texture of leaves and petals—a grounding gesture that pulls me down out of the buzzing clouds of abstraction and worry. Or I have simply folded my arms upon the sill, laid down my head, and allowed myself to be borne away on a cloud of fragrance. This is my sacred garden.

That all gardens are sacred I readily admit. By extension, so is every inch of gloriously wild, bitterly neglected, or concrete-buried land all over this volatile garden we call Earth. But we humans are particularizing creatures. Certain stretches and corners lay special claim to the spirit, become our soul places. These sacred gardens seem to exist apart from, if not the seasons, then the artificial hyperkinetics of clock time. Their purity of purpose resonates, stilling all other activities but those that ritualize the awareness of being. Thus in soul places we may walk or sit or even exercise our bodies, but our skittering minds come home and settle themselves. Here our hearts and senses, which have been so tense from self-protection, can open like water lilies. Here, away from the anticommunicative whirring and bleeps of faxes, phone calls, pagers, and e-mail, we can receive—as naturally as the sound of one person whispering to another—precisely that truth which the living earth would reveal to us in that moment.

The quest for the sacred garden connotes the mystique of other lands and ancient times. One thinks of the Hanging Gardens of Babylon, the lush entanglements of Machu Picchu, and the carefully ordered hedges of a French parterre. Perhaps you have murmured in delight as you wandered the Butchart Gardens of Victoria Island or felt some lost aspect of pleasure and serenity returned to you as you trailed your fingers through the fountain of the Tuileries. Still, propinquity is not to be underrated. The daily realm requires its sacred places, too.

Just as you may uncover within your own complexity or distraction a center of peace and clarity, let your quest for soul places lead you to a sacred garden close at hand. How will you know this place? Not by its size, for it may extend the length and breadth of the land you live on or it may be no bigger than the humble window box. Indeed, it may occupy a physical space no bigger than a terrarium or ceramic pot. What matters is the space it occupies in your unlimited heart. Look, then, for that part of the garden, that grove or single tree, that kitchen step bordered by mint or godetia, that unique site to which you are most attracted, most likely to stop and just *be*. Find and acknowledge that special place.

This leads us to another important aspect of the sacred garden: namely, that it is a place of repose rather than of labor. Naturally, there will be some maintenance, but the focus should be on refreshing your soul, not deadheading the petunias and mending the drip irrigation. That's why, although I encounter wonder wherever I ramble, the window box is my particular sacred garden. It is ideally suited for stopping me in my tracks and gathering my scattered mental meanderings into a single bouquet of attention. Here there is no rototilling to be done, and any weeds are easily dispensed with or, more likely, accepted and contemplated. A mere handful of seeds tossed in on a good day may, by the inevitable arrival of a morning of bleak discouragement, be blooming to spectacular effect.

I like, too, that window boxes are places where the outside garden enters into the house, a reminder of the constant intersection of spirit and matter. Many a warm summer night I've lain in bed, floating in that delicate juncture where dream world meets the waking world, as through the open window the scents of lavender, stock, and night-blooming jasmine wash the air of all anxiety. The word *window* is etymologically *wind-eye*, and what is wind, that singing invisibility, but an aspect of spirit, the spirit to which we refer whenever we say we are *in-spired*, the spirit that breathes in and out of us in every respiration of our lives. Thus my window becomes an eye watching for spirit even as I sleep, while the flowers of the window box invite, welcome, and respire with that spirit, too.

Now let's say that you have already created your sacred garden. The real trick may be learning how to *be* in that sacred space. The return to paradise on a daily basis, given the extreme demands and frenetic rhythm of this age, seems challenged at every step. For most home gardeners, its re-creation has become an activity reserved for the weekend, and while the very rigors involved satisfy many practitioners of this sacred art, for others gardening soon devolves into a chore. Given limited time and imaginative ambitions, one can easily get so caught up in making and maintaining the garden that one forgets to *live* in the garden. When was the last time you plopped down on the soft grass, leaned against the thickening birch tree, or watched the sunset from an artful arrangement of Adirondack chairs?

When I was a journalist in Ireland, I once interviewed a woman who had created a backyard garden of such splendor that first-time visitors invariably responded with a gasp of amazement. This lavish, rambling garden, dense with shady nooks, sunlit vantage points, and pathways leading to hidden territories of delight, was located on a former wasteland. So thick had been the brambles, creepers, and other invasives that not even surveyors had detected the presence of an underground stream that rose up at one point like one of Ireland's holy wells and babbled, unheard, along the far end of the property. Now it sang to all and was adorned with a red Japanese footbridge. As I walked the land, aware that I was in the presence of a wizard, albeit one with apple cheeks and freckles, I listened to inspiring accounts of reclamation and innovation. Here, surely, was the lost Eden.

Then I asked the woman whether early morning, midday, or just before sunset was her favorite time to sit and admire the garden. She looked at me as if my head had just toppled off and rolled under the shrubbery. "Oh, I never sit in the garden," she said.

"Never?" I pressed.

"Never," she said.

"Well, then," I mumbled disbelievingly, "when do you like to just stroll about and look at it all?"

"I don't do any strolling about," said she, her sharp tone putting that activity on a par with dancing on tabletops at the local pub. Then she softened, realizing she was in the presence of a horticultural ninny. "I just work in the garden. From sunup to sundown. I can't stand to do nothing, and there's always plenty to be done."

I think of that woman now, years hence, and wonder if at this very moment, eight hours ahead of me by the clock, she is still busily working away, still disinclined to pause for even a moment and witness the beauty that she is co-creating. I hope not. *O Patron Saint of Indolence, discover her!* I think, too, of the four-by-four-foot porch at the back of a century-old house I lived in once in Galway. It was little more than a roofless stone closet but I lined it with diminutive terraces of potted plants and curtained the walls with trailing vines, leaving just enough room for a straight-backed wooden chair. On summer days, when the sun would float like an escaped balloon late into the dazzling night, I would sit there reading poetry or just staring into the flowers, whose names I did not know but whose every blossom closed around the secrets of my heart. I was in paradise.

Perhaps, then, paradise requires not splendor per se but only witness to experience it. That being so, we need to set down the rake and pause in our great bustling plans every now and then and simply be present to our garden as it is. In this way we tend that garden within, that unnamable center that knows its own deep thirst, its own longing for light and nurture, that place which may lie fallow for the longest time only to surprise us one day like a suddenly glimpsed field of brilliant flowers.

Now it's one thing to pause during the weekend, especially if one is inclined to be out in the garden anyway. But what about the rest of the week? Perhaps you wake before dawn and commute a great distance to a busy office, where lunch is a hurried affair in your cubicle, at a crowded bagelry, or en route to the next appointment. Then it's home again to another round of responsibilities and soon to bed. How often can one as busy as you return to some green and mystic place?

I say, more often than you might think.

The famous visionary Black Elk once spoke of his habit of greeting each morning by stepping outside, letting his bare feet touch the wet grass, literally reconnecting with the earth, and singing a prayer of gratitude for the day's arrival. Whenever I do this, I find that it is virtually impossible to have a bad day, for I have first reminded myself what a gift it is to be given this earth in the first place. No matter how busy you are, there is time for this ritual for it takes only a moment, and it is a moment that can transform the tenor of the day. If the weather rules against walking out barefoot, you might simply remove a mitten long enough to pat the earth or feel the bark of a tree, but do not omit this powerful act of touching. So, too, if you are not inclined to sing on Monday mornings, then whisper, or simply stand in silence. If your garden is indoors, adapt your ritual accordingly. Spend a moment, as if at a lighted candle in a shrine, with one or more plants by the window, perhaps facing east toward the rising sun or searching the sky for dawdling stars. Let your gratitude announce itself to the earth.

When you come home in the evening, allow yourself some time with the garden, but don't get right to work on it. Pull up a chair by the window and watch what the winter sunset does to the land. In summer, change out of that suit and go sit on the grass, the way you used to do as a kid just home from school.

Don't scowl at the weeds; see if there's a little frog or interesting bug hiding in them. Retreat to your favorite corner. The underused narrow margin of land at the side of many tract houses makes an ideal secret garden. Keep it low-maintenance with potted plants or fragrant floral shrubs that add to your privacy. Place in it a single statue or ornamental object that has meaning for you. Sit and breathe, giving yourself a moment to just be.

Find your sacred gardens in the everyday, and tend them well. Breathe with them and bless them. They will grow, I assure you, spilling over the ordinary like a luxuriant cascade of morning glories. Seed and nurture the most mundane aspect of your life until, in ways you never imagined, it breaks irrepressibly into blossom.

SACRED
GARDENS ARE
EVERYWHERE

The great problem is bringing life back into the wasteland, where people live inauthentically.

—*Joseph Campbell,*
A Joseph Campbell Companion

GARDENING
AT THE OFFICE

Finding paradise in the workplace is not without its difficulties. In my editorial days, I worked in an office located in one of California's most beautiful counties. Tourists came from all over the world to view the spectacular Monterey coastline with its marine sanctuary, to hike the scenic trails, and to view the hillsides' annual display of wildflowers. Yet nowhere within walking distance of our office could you ramble down a path or find a park. Dozens of architecturally ambitious buildings stood shoulder to shoulder around a kind of square, like well-dressed strangers at an executive convention. This square, however, was no verdant plaza, only a moat of busy streets bordering the parking lots of several upscale malls. Here and there, trees stood prisoner in concrete boxes, the narrow rims of which discouraged loitering.

In the office itself was a pleasant-enough lunchroom with Saltillo tiles and enormous windows that made the overhead fluorescents superfluous. One floor up was a rooftop terrace with a few scattered plastic chairs. Employees who did not wish to rehash the latest episodes of TV sitcoms or find their lunch break turned into an impromptu editorial meeting could retreat to this aerie, there to gaze upon a green valley floor — mostly farmland plotted with developers' signs — or to look longingly at the wilder mountains, beyond which lay Big Sur and the Pacific. It was a view to savor, but refreshing as this was to eyes strained by the umpteenth batch of revisions in nine-point type, the body longed for something more. Hands that have gardened over the weekend do not lose their hunger for the earth on all the days between.

Happily, even the most urban office offers a pathway back into Eden. Over the years I have discovered that you need not relegate your healing connection with nature and the garden to the weekend, only to be deprived of it from Monday to Friday. The following suggestions are just a few of the ways to find gardens in the workplace. Like runaway sweet-pea vines, a few ideas may be a little off the wall. On the other hand, wouldn't it be nice to stop and smell the roses even while you're on the job?

51

GARDENING AT
THE OFFICE

- *Keep a nature journal.* Yes, that's right, at the office. To those of you not employed at the local aquarium or nursery, the notion may sound absurd. However, it works. I began keeping just such a journal while working at the publishing house. It consisted of a burgeoning collection of index cards, each of which bore a hastily penciled sentence or two about something I had observed, whether on the way to work, from my window, or during a lunch break. One day I quickly cataloged from memory some flowers I had seen displayed outside a produce market. Another time I wrote about five birds in the golden maple tree of the adjacent parking lot, finding a connection that day between their comic squabbling and the confused longing of my own five senses. Over the months I compiled descriptions of the changing sky and weather, a list of cafés decorated with real (not artificial) plants, quotations from nature poetry as well as from the marvelous children's literature that came through our publishing house, plants sighted around the office that transcended the generic green-leaves-in-a-pot seasonal variations in the landscape fronting certain office buildings, memories of gardens past or gardens visited during business travel, even a guide to the surprising variety of flowers that shouldered their way up through cracks in the sidewalk. The prize entry of my collection was a descriptive listing of parks, nature preserves, and secret gardens that one could reach — though only, alas, by car — during a lunch break.

While the journal took only moments a day to compile, the benefits to my spirit were enormous. The French say of good gardeners not that they have a green thumb but that they have *un main vert*, a green hand. With every entry I penciled in I was keeping my hand green and subsequently nurturing the heart, even in the midst of computers, stark white partitions, and fluorescent lighting. The journal became a verdant plot that I could harvest, as appropriate, whenever I wrote copy, experienced a block in creativity, or simply needed a better stress reliever than vending machine candy.

The format for your office nature journal is up to you. Just use index cards, as I did, or treat yourself to a beautiful blank book. An illustrated daybook, such as those published by the Sierra Club, the Audubon Society, and other nature-oriented groups, is another option. Your office gardening can bear real fruit if you look for calendars whose publishers donate a share of the profits to nature conservancy, homeless garden projects, or the protection of endangered species.

• *Start a gardening club at work.* Chances are that many of your colleagues have wrought wonders on their home territory, so why spend your days deprived of natural beauty?

Invite interested persons to meet twice a month during lunch; then do a little brainstorming. You might ask the company for a small budget or matching fund that would allow you to replace the artificial ficus and shriveled philodendron with something more imaginative. Offer to maintain the office garden on a rotating basis, say, on casual Fridays.

Far from adding to your workload, you may discover that devoting an occasional break to repotting a plant or tending an African violet boosts your energy. Good focus sites for your office garden club are the employee lunchroom, a courtyard or patio, and the various points at which people enter the building. Exchange cuttings of indoor plants to spruce up each other's desks, as well as cuttings, seeds, and tips for gardening at home. Share gardening articles or subscribe as a group to your favorite magazines. Keep a bulletin board on which to post home garden photos, news of community garden activities, and ideas for the next meeting.

• *Change your lunchtime migration patterns.* How often have you escaped the din of the lunchroom only to end up in the din of an eatery that walloped your digestive system or wreaked havoc with your budget? Because there were no open spaces within walking distance of my office, a group of us would sometimes carpool to a park overlooking the ocean. Having worked together all morning, we might wander off into our solitudes, meeting back at the car at an appointed time. A stroll among the cypresses, or along a path bordered with sea holly, works wonders on the psyche. Other times we sought out local parks, gardens, and undemanding nature trails. (You don't want to go back to the office in a sweat or festooned with burrs.) When necessary, we negotiated flex time for our excursions.

- *Go to the mall.* If none of the above are available to you, don't despair. Here's another idea, although I offer it advisedly. In fact, it's something I thought I'd never suggest. Now hold on, it can't be just any mall. No subterranean caverns with dueling Muzak and eerie lighting. However, if, failing all other choices, you know of an outdoor shopping center nearby with a garden—by which I mean more than a few concrete bunkers jammed with spindly snapdragons—try it. At one well-known shopping center in Monterey, the nondescript landscaping was restored to bucolic splendor by garden designer Elizabeth Murray, author of *Monet's Passion.* Everything Ms. Murray garnered from her working sojourn in the artist's home of Giverny, France, is given glorious expression in this most unlikely setting.

    In my own area, the only relief to the granite and asphalt topography was to be found at a shopping center known as the Barnyard, where raised mounds bursting with lavish blooms graced the terraced plazas. Many an afternoon I sat on one of the wooden benches, contentedly nibbling my tuna sandwich in the company of matilija poppies, larkspur, fragrant herbs, and my favorite bells of Ireland. Like many another office drone, I envied the hard-working gardener there. Not only did he have nature for his office, but he could bring his dog along as well. Such a deal.

The trick, of course, is to remember that you aren't there to shop. Okay, so *occasionally* I gave in to temptation, picking up novels and books of poetry at the legendary Thunderbird Book Store. In the main, however, I limited my indulgence to inhaling the perfume of flowers and watching the monarch butterflies wander by.

Some other sources of urban gardens that you might not have thought of include libraries, hospitals, hotels, and college campuses. The most important thing is to reaffirm your connection with nature each and every day. In our culture, smokers are outdoors more than most of their colleagues. Yet as living embodiments of nature, everyone needs fresh air, sunlight, and the green nourishment of good earth. So read that brief on the balcony (wind factor permitting). Pass up the stale doughnut and savor a juicy organic peach in season. Take a moment to turn your golden pothos toward the sun. Dare to grow an exotic orchid. Treat your desk to a vase of fresh-cut tulips.

Many a paradise is hiding in plain sight. The earth itself is so much with us that, curiously, we may forget it for days on end. Yet how it bears us up, spinning us faithfully through the

GARDENING
BY HEART

days, whether we are mindful of it or not. We separate our-selves from it by a thousand means and materials, but the earth, for all our arrogance, never shrinks back from us. The gravity of earth pulls us in, literally, like a compassionate par-ent embracing a sulky child. Think about that the next time you feel enclosed by all that is human-made. Feel the earth under the carpet and the concrete, letting the tension of the workday fall from your body as you do, and just for a moment return to the simplicity of Eden.

Summer

FLOWERING

LIKE

WILD

At other times, I would sleep among the rhododendrons and rocks in the wilder part of the grounds of Howth Castle. After a while my father said I must stay indoors half the night, meaning that I should get some sleep in my bed.

—*William Butler Yeats*,
Reveries Over Childhood and Youth

EATING, SLEEPING, AND LIVING IN THE GARDEN

In my childhood home of what was then the rural-to-wild environs of Thousand Oaks, California, the backyard was another living room. On Saturdays and after school, forgoing cartoons on television, my brothers, sisters, and I raided the orchards and sculpted the tall grass of the fields into tunnels, forts, and cottages. My older brother, Michael, who went on to develop Virtual Reality at NASA, helped my mother create garden environments, including hidden gardens-within-the-garden and elaborate terraced pathways bordered by as many rocks as a shovel could unearth. My sister Carolyn and I would imitate this grandeur on a smaller scale, creating maze-like walkways to our playhouse and filling the windowsills with pickle jars of roses and geraniums. My younger brothers, John and Tom, had their tree houses. The "babies," Margie and Erin, ran a tree-stump shop that purportedly sold fresh strawberries, although the stock tended to run low and the proprietors had suspiciously red-stained faces.

I have a memory of my oldest sister, Kathleen—so beautiful and brainy, it's a wonder anything was left over for the rest of us—sitting in the green shade of the patio with two or three admirers from high school, one of whom christened me Charlie Horse. I did tend to hang around at such times when a young man might be hoping to steal a kiss without witnesses. However, having then no inkling of the implications, I reveled in my moniker, even sharing it with my most cherished toy, a jet-black rocking horse with flaring red nostrils that gave its vinyl form a certain apocalyptic glory. I dragged Charlie Horse into groves of almond trees and across all the flower beds, as if I were truly galloping the length of the Golden State.

When we ate outside, which was often, elegance prevailed. My mother would have had it no other way, reasoning that dining outdoors was no mere expedient but rather a potent return to the source of wonder. We would lay tablecloths: lavender to catch the reflection of the summer solstice moon, red check for the way it glowed with the hardy last rays of sunset, or perhaps just a simple white, the lace of which swirled like images half remembered from a dream.

There would be flowers on the table and flowers all around us. Salads and fresh-cooked corn from the garden. Ice cream that had been made from our own peaches, the crank of the old mixer having been turned, throughout the day, by eight or more pairs of hands. "Bless us, O Lord, and these Thy gifts, which we are about to receive from Thy bounty." The word *Lord* got mixed up in my head with images of medieval knights, glimpsed in old copies of *My Book House,* as well as with the lard Mom used in homemade tortillas. But I knew what *bounty* meant. This was it.

In the garden, anything could happen. One night my mother suddenly got up in the middle of an alfresco dessert course, retrieved some gray and brown paints from her studio, and came running back. Entranced by the play of candlelight that cast the diners' forms onto the wall behind them, Mom told everyone present to hold still while she filled in the silhouettes. What looked somewhat awkward and lumpish during the day took on an eerily magical aspect by candlelight. Visitors would suddenly do a double-take as they noticed the extra—and apparently independent—shadows. After our parents died, the shadows took on a poignant quality, stirring memories of Dad's way of leaning into another great story, as well as Mom's enduring talent for drawing one's attention to the moment.

On very warm nights, we slept outside. I suppose this must have started back before air-conditioning became a California commonplace. Still, many of us liked it so much that we continued the practice long after the need for it ended. To this day, no summer is complete unless I have spent at least one night of it, and hopefully many more, falling asleep with delicious slowness under the stars. It is a pleasure no gardener or garden-lover should miss. As a child, I remember the safety I felt in that circle of dreaming, listening, or whispering forms. My parents would tell us stories, never fairy tales—those we found easily enough in books—but the stories that only a parent can tell. Anecdotes of their own childhood, adolescence, and—impossible for my siblings and me to fully comprehend—the days of their marriage when it was *just the two of them.*

If certain details of the stories fade, the sight or scent of plants that flourished in our garden is enough to revive their essence. I see a bottlebrush tree and vicariously recall my mother at age nine, sitting on somebody's porch steps with her younger brothers. They are waiting for the Ladies Auxiliary to depart the Methodist church across the street. Once the good ladies appear, Mom and her brothers will blow talcum powder through rolled-up paper, hoping to look like young toughs dragging on cigarettes.

I breathe in the scent of honeysuckle and hear my father's

account of meeting my mother at the officers' club at Luke Air Force Field in Phoenix, Arizona. How, having caught sight of her honey-red hair and startling green eyes earlier in the day, he went to that night's dance and waited outside, hoping she would show up. Which she did, two hours later.

"Where on earth have you been? I've been waiting for you all night," he declared.

"And what did *you* think, Mom?" we would ask. We knew the answer already, but our call-and-response was a key element of the storytelling ritual.

"I thought, Who the heck is this? And that he was handsome."

Later that night at the dance, allowing no one to cut in on them, although many tried, our father told our mother that he was "much older"—twenty-nine instead of twenty-three—and had a glass eye, which in fact he did not.

"I wanted to find out if she could love me for myself," our father explained.

"And what did *you* think, Mom?"

"That he was crazy. And handsome."

Three weeks later they married. Twenty, thirty, forty years later, on every anniversary, they would ask each other with a grin, "Well, do you think it's going to last?"

Once my son asked me, "If you could go back to any time in history, what period would you choose?" I told him I would go back to those nights dining in the garden. "*That* isn't history," he protested. Oh, but it is.

GARDENING
BY HEART

Whether you set a lavish table in a grove or simply pull a few chairs and any excuse for a table out onto a plant-filled balcony, it is in a garden that the fruits of the garden can best be savored. Besides, when was the last time you heard someone reminiscing fondly about the magical evenings they spent eating take-out pizza in front of the TV?

PATCHWORK TOMATOES

One of the easiest ways to prepare the bountiful tomatoes of summer is to serve them raw. What makes this dish special is the combination of different varieties and colors. Many heirloom and exotic varieties are as easy to grow as generic hybrids, and the taste is beyond comparison. So along with the usual ruby-red beefsteaks, include such stunners as Lemon Yellows, Russian Black Krims, Green Zebras, Cherokee Purples, and old-fashioned cherry tomatoes like Yellow Plum, Green Grape, and Red Robin.

2 to 4 pounds of heirloom tomatoes (in as many
   varieties as you can find—or harvest—including
   plenty of cherry tomatoes)
sea salt, to taste
1 bunch of basil or parsley, chopped

Slice all but the cherry tomatoes. Fan out the slices on a platter in concentric rings, combining the various colors into a pattern that pleases your eye. Loosely dot the slices with the cherry tomatoes. Season with a little bit of sea salt and garnish with parsley or basil. Skip the salad dressing and let the eloquent tastes speak for themselves.

MEMORY-OF-SUMMER ROAST TOMATO SAUCE

Folk musician Greg Brown sings of a grandmother who practiced the art of storing "summer in a jar," stirring its potent magic into the cheering meals of winter. You can practice this art with very little fuss by roasting down your summer tomatoes for sauce and then sealing them up and freezing them to use in winter soups and other dishes.

ripe tomatoes (as many as you can fit into a glass
   baking dish)
2 to 3 tablespoons of olive oil
½ to 1 cup of chopped onion, red or yellow
2 to 4 cloves of crushed garlic
½ cup of fresh basil (or ¼ cup of chopped rosemary)
½ cup of fresh parsley
sea salt and pepper, to taste

1. Cut the tomatoes in half and scoop out the seeds.
2. Place the tomatoes in the baking dish. Drizzle with olive oil.

3. Mix in the onions, garlic, and herbs. Add salt and pepper.

4. Roast at 375 degrees for at least an hour. You will know the sauce is done when the tomatoes have collapsed and begun to caramelize.

5. Freeze to keep.

MEMORY-OF-SUMMER TOMATO SOUP

1 10-ounce can of condensed tomato soup

2 14-ounce cans of chicken or vegetable broth

½ cup of Memory-of-Summer Roast Tomato Sauce
   (see preceding recipe)

1 tablespoon of honey

a dash of lemon pepper

sea salt, as desired

sour cream and chopped herbs for garnish

1. Heat the soup, but do not add water.

2. Add two cans of broth.

3. When the soup is simmering, stir in the tomato sauce.

4. Stir in the honey. Season with salt and pepper.

5. Garnish with a dollop of sour cream and your favorite chopped herbs. Basil, tarragon, and herbes de Provence (recipe follows) are all good choices.

HERBES DE PROVENCE

One of the great pleasures of the garden is using your own herbs. Once you've seasoned roast potatoes with sprigs of fresh rosemary, there's no going back to those overpriced little jars of savorless particles. Making your own herbes de Provence is a marvelous way to harvest your herbal bounty. You can mix this with extra-virgin olive oil and balsamic vinegar for a terrific salad dressing, sprinkle it on pasta, and add it to soups. Simply combine as many of the following as you have on hand.

1 tablespoon of crushed lavender buds

1 tablespoon of chopped rosemary

2 tablespoons each of the following, chopped: basil, thyme, marjoram, savory, and chervil

That's it. If summer brings you an abundance of these herbs, consider drying and freezing several batches to use throughout the winter and to give as holiday gifts.

ROAST CHICKEN WITH ROSEMARY MARINADE

This marinade has the taste of my mother's garden. It's also a great time-saver and is therefore ideal for the busy person who likes to entertain. Whip it up in minutes; marinate the main dish overnight.

4 chicken quarters or thighs

8 cloves of garlic, minced

2 oranges, cut in half

2 lemons, cut in half

4 three-inch sprigs of rosemary

3 tablespoons of olive oil

1. Ream the orange and lemon halves into a bowl. Strain the juice to remove the seeds or, if you like the pulp for texture as I do, just spoon the seeds out.

2. Add the minced garlic.

3. In a glass baking dish, set each chicken part on top of a sprig of rosemary. Pour the garlic and citrus mixture over the chicken. Cover with plastic wrap and chill for up to 24 hours, turning the chicken occasionally.

To cook, lightly drizzle olive oil over the chicken. Cook for about 45 minutes to one hour at 500 degrees. No, that's not a misprint. That's a superb method I picked up from Frances McCullough and Barbara Will, authors of *Great Food Without Fuss*. This method ensures the tenderest chicken. To check for doneness, pierce chicken with a sharp knife. The juice should run clear, and the meat should have lost its pinkness.

Tips

- Purchase your chicken from a natural foods store that does not use antibiotics or artificial preservatives.

- Keep the accompaniments simple: salad, a loaf of bread, and fresh fruit and sorbet for dessert.
- This marinade works well with vegetables. Try a mixture of summer squash and fresh corn cut from the cob. In winter, combine turnips, carrots, garlic, and whole onions. Roast the marinated vegetables at 375 degrees until tender (about 1½ hours). Add a splash of balsamic vinegar. Serve with *pappardelle* noodles, polenta, or wild rice.

BEAUTIFUL BEAN SOUP

Anyone who's ever used those packets of dried-up beans and high-sodium "flavorizer" might dismiss bean soup as utterly boring. There's nothing boring about it, however, when you grow your own beans. These varieties rival the beauty of precious stones:

- Black Turtle, beans the color of midnight, have a chocolaty flavor ideal for tomato-based soups and chilis.
- Jacob's Cattle, tiny white pebbles brindled with maroon, are hearty and sweet, perfect for stews and baked beans.
- Borlotto, an Italian variety easily recognized in the pod, turns rosy-red and cream. Serve chilled in a winter salad with a fruity vinaigrette.
- Speckled Yellow Eye, plump white ovals with a daub of yellow, can be boiled plain and jazzed up with a dash of olive oil and chopped sage.

- Vermont Cranberry, glossy cranberry-colored beans, add color and flavor to more generic beans.
- Low's Champion, oblong beans the color of red wine with white eyes, can be layered among other beans in glass jars to give as gifts.

Note: Two reliable sources of unusual shelling beans are The Cook's Garden (P.O. Box 5010, Hodges, SC 29653) and Shepherd's Garden Seeds (30 Irene Street, Torrington, CT 06790).

1 or 2 leeks, trimmed

3 big cloves of garlic, sliced

1 tablespoon of strong olive oil or butter

½ cup each of chopped carrots and celery

1 cup of dried shelling beans, which have soaked
    overnight

enough water or stock to cover the beans by a few
    inches, about 8 cups

1 fresh bay leaf

sea salt and pepper to taste

herbs and garnishes as desired

1. Cut the leeks in half and wash thoroughly, as they can retain a lot of soil between layers. Chop into thin slices.

2. Using a large soup pot, sauté the leeks and garlic in the

oil or butter on medium heat until they are soft and translucent.

3. Add carrots, celery, and beans. Immediately add the water or stock. Bring the soup to a boil, then down to a gentle simmer. Add the bay leaf. Cover the pot and cook on low heat for 2 hours.

4. Just before serving, add salt, pepper, and, if desired, additional amounts of your chosen herb. If desired, garnish with chopped walnuts, parsley, or tomatoes. Serves 4 to 6.

Variations

- In place of carrots and celery, try ½ cup each of chopped winter squash and turnips.
- In place of bay leaf, try chopped curry plant or winter savory.

HEART-OF-THE-GARDEN ICED TEA

It's always seemed strange to me that so few California houses have front porches. We certainly have the summers for them. While patios ensure your solitude, there's nothing like a porch as a way to establish a sense of local community. When my sister Carolyn and her family lived in Thousand Oaks she made a point of sitting out on the porch every summer evening. Soon she was on cordial terms with every child and parent in the neighborhood and was instrumental in midwifing many friendships between people who'd lived for years as complete strangers.

Of course, it helped that Carolyn always offered the best iced tea this side of paradise. Through the open screen door wafted the scents of homemade spaghetti sauce, soups from the garden, and cinnamon cookies. Her house was definitely the place to slow your stride and say hello.

Whether you're socializing on the porch or taking your ease after a day of gardening, making Heart-of-the-Garden Iced Tea couldn't be easier. Simply supplement your regular pitchers of decaffeinated tea with sprigs of herbs. Some great combinations include:

- Peach tea with pineapple mint
- Decaffeinated organic black tea with cinnamon basil
- Apple tea with chamomile
- Orange or raspberry tea with lemon balm or lemon verbena
- Rosehip tea with lavender

If you want to get really fancy, freeze borage flowers in ice cubes and float them in the tea. (For more about borage, read on.)

BORAGE, THE ULTIMATE GARNISH

No herb garden should be without borage, a fuzzy green bush that produces voluminous amounts of edible flowers. The flowers are sky-blue beauties that taste a bit like cucumber. To harvest them, simply grasp the black center between forefinger and thumb and lift it off.

One cutting of borage will soon run riot, if you like that sort of thing. (I do.) Otherwise, contain it as you would mint. As a rich source of organic minerals and a deterrent to tomato worm, borage is the ideal companion plant for tomatoes. Best of all, the unusual color of the borage flower makes it a highly dramatic garnish. For example, you can:

- Freeze it in ice cubes for drinks.
- Mix it into a plain green salad with peppery nasturtium petals.
- Scatter it on thinly sliced, layered, and marinated cucumber slices.
- Toss it over fresh tomatoes.
- Use it to decorate a lightly glazed angel food cake.
- Add it to strawberry cheesecake for the Fourth of July.
- Use it to liven up old favorites, such as deviled eggs and potato salad.

Our attitude toward plants is a singularly narrow one. If we see any immediate utility in a plant we foster it. If for any reason we find its presence undesirable or merely a matter of indifference, we may condemn it to destruction forthwith.

—Rachel Carson,
Silent Spring

A WEED BY ANY OTHER NAME

A European visitor to my garden remarks on the beautiful flowers, "especially that one over there." I search in vain among the salvias, cosmos, and other blossoms trying to figure out which flower she means. Is it the mauve pincushion flowers? The nigella? The cranesbill geranium?

"No," she says, "that creamy white flower with the pink markings. See it?"

"Oh, *that*," I say dismissively. "That's a weed, that's nothing." Picture the wicked stepmother of the fairy tale as she grudgingly acknowledges Cinderella.

This particular Cinderella is convolvulus, which in its refined state we call the morning glory. Because it's a "weed," I've stopped seeing it. Now that I take the time to look at it, it *is* beautiful, an elegant interloper mingling with the garden's invited guests.

But it's too late. I've declared it nothing and my visitor has obligingly picked up that disapproval. As we continue our tour of the garden, she no longer seems to notice it. I have destroyed it with a single word.

The term *weed* comes from the Old English *weod*, meaning "any herb or small plant." According to that definition, the average ornamental garden is almost exclusively weeds, with a few trees and shrubs thrown in for contrast. Today, however, the word is reserved for those plants whose evolutionary hardiness has earned them the bitter resentment of gardeners everywhere. Curious and enduring, their purpose all but forgotten, weeds are the cockroaches of the plant kingdom.

Even some of the most mild-mannered organic gardening books roll out the battle rhetoric when it comes to weeds. "Top Ten Tactics for Wiping Out Infiltrators!" declares one. "Move 'em out! Choke 'em! Cut off their heads!" suggests another.

Clearly the most peaceable, cheery gardeners have their shadow side, and weeds bring it into play.

I too have experienced a lust to see chlorophyll spilled at the mention of certain weeds. Pampas grass, featured in numerous catalogs as a prized ornamental, poses a greater threat to California chaparral than wildfire, whose range and speed it rivals. Far from playing well with others, pampas grass wants every field for itself. For this reason, native plant lovers in our area dig up this obnoxious beauty wherever it appears.

At the same time, I have come to revise my attitude toward certain other uninvited plants. Come tiptoe through the weeds with me and I'll show you what I mean.

☙

Those dandelions peppering the south forty? Those aren't just weeds, those are nutrients. Dandelions are loaded with vitamins A and C. They are also rich in iron. They pull it out of the soil at about triple the rate of other plants. Admittedly, this doesn't endear them to their botanical neighbors, but it does suggest why you might think twice before adding chemical insult to injury.

Instead of wasting their ill-gotten nutrient booty, put it to good use. One way is to toss the bitter leaves, the flowers, even the diced roots into a green salad. Your liver, kidneys, and digestive and circulatory systems will reap the benefits. In Italy, no *insalata di campo*, or salad of wild greens, would be complete without a generous helping of tender *foglie del soffione*, otherwise known as dandelion leaves, to give it bite.

If you don't care to eat weeds, thank you very much, then at least invest those riches back into your garden. Generally, adding weeds to your compost is considered a no-no. The truth is, really experienced gardeners do it all the time. You just need to make sure that your compost pile heats up enough to kill off the weed seeds. You can always start a second experimental compost pile if you're not sure.

You can also make dandelions into a kind of tea, which, if sprayed on your plants, will help keep hungry insects away. (Ever notice how perfect and unbitten the dandelions are as they stand to attention beside clusters of limp and ragged cosmos or petunias?) Or use the tea as a fertilizer to boost the nutrient levels of the soil. Be sure to sieve the seeds out first by pouring it through a fine-mesh strainer.

One note of caution: Don't eat any dandelions that come from a chemically treated lawn. Better yet, stop treating the lawn. Best of all, tear up the lawn and invite the native plants back in—many of which just happen to include what some folks call weeds.

Flax, for instance, a plant whose seeds have been discovered in ancient Egyptian tombs, has been routinely pulled out of flower beds by gardeners. For years, I promptly uprooted its tall quilled spikes of aquamarine while vainly attempting to get some blue into my poppy-gold garden via costly mail-order flowers. Eventually patience, or more likely laziness, caught up with me, and as the mail-order specimens withered into the ground, the flax produced perfect sky-blue flowers. I have since noticed flax for sale at native plant nurseries and learned that it is of great value to local songbirds. I have also learned to look for blue flowers not among the pages of catalogs but out in the open where they grow like — well, weeds. Think of such locals as Pacific Coast iris, the night-sky blue of lupine, the cobalt of wild lilac and many salvias, or that highway rambler, blue-eyed grass.

All too often, weeding escalates into denuding an area of all plant life with which we are unfamiliar or which does not conform to a stereotypical garden image. Here's a common scenario in California's chaparral regions. A couple buys a house and decides to clear the surrounding lot of "scrub." A bulldozer is hired or goats are brought in, and away goes the rugged blend of manzanita, sage, young oak, and a host of native flowers. When the ground is completely bare, the couple gets into their car, drives to the nearest nursery, and looks for landscaping advice. "What grows well here?" they ask. Guess.

In an age of vanishing nature, it's imperative to *read before you weed*. Get yourself a field guide to native plants or invite someone who knows them to take you on a tour of your own garden. Taking samples of mystery plants to a meeting of your local native plant society is another way to find out what your garden grows.

The rule of read before you weed is particularly important when it comes to "ugly duckling" plants. Milkweed, no catalog beauty-contest winner, is another native that California gardeners have unknowingly stripped from the soil to make way for more elegant cottage gardens. Now let's say that the gardeners in question are hoping to attract butterflies to their weed-free garden. They scour the catalogs for just the right plants, place their orders, and charge up the old credit card. A season later, the garden appears to be flourishing. But where are the butterflies? That's funny, there were lots of them when the land was nothing but weeds.

It turns out that the monarch butterfly is totally dependent on milkweed during the larval stage. After eating the egg from which it hatched, the larva starts looking around for milkweed leaves. If it finds them, it grows so rapidly in the next two weeks that it sheds its skin four times and achieves 3,000 times its birth weight. If the larva does not find milkweed, the gardener will not find monarch butterflies.

Another underrated native is coyote bush. Fortunately for native plant lovers, the resilient coyote bush is frequently found in disturbed areas performing the role of healer. In the shade of the coyote bush one often finds the delicate seedlings of other herbs and shrubs making their way back. More than two hundred kinds of insects are dependent on this plant, which in turn attracts songbirds. If ever a weed lived in service to beauty, it's coyote bush. I love it best as late autumn turns to winter, when its fluffy white seed pods create the illusion of light snowfall.

And speaking of snow . . . when I was a child celebrating Christmas in what was then wild oak-studded land in Southern California, my brothers and sisters and I even made snowmen from weeds. We would capture three bleached-white tumbleweeds—no easy task as they rolled through the fields, faster than galloping horses and nearly as big—stack them, and add a wool scarf and eyes of barbecue coal. A weedman he might be, but to us he was always the best snowman ever, and each year Mom and Dad would admire our handiwork as if we had re-created Michelangelo's David.

🌱

Many of the weeds banished from our gardens are actually herbs, each with its own rich lore.

Take mugwort. Elizabethan women slipped this aromatic plant under their pillows to induce prophetic visions of their true loves. Some Native Americans still use mugwort instead of sage in their sweat lodges. Even people who have never heard of mugwort may have tasted it, since it is often used to flavor apéritifs.

But mugwort has a brass-tacks practical side as well. When not found as a prized member of the herbalist's garden, it thrives alongside poison oak. That's good, because the juice of mugwort is just the thing to help break up the irritating oils of poison oak should you happen to get some on you. An infusion of mugwort has also been said to alleviate everything from indigestion to depression, while a poultice of mugwort reduces swelling in a sprained ankle.

One of the most hated of the garden's uninvited guests is the stinging nettle, another herb. You may not know it on sight, but you sure know it on contact. The merest touch, and dozens of tiny welts rise up like angry yeomen at the point of assault. What you've done is to break the brittle needlelike tubes of fluid contained in each and every hair of the plant. Some gardeners claim that taking firm hold of the plant, rather than brushing against it, actually *prevents* the hairs from breaking open, but my sense of adventure goes only so far.

On the other hand, preferably the one wearing the heavy glove, nettles make one of the most nutritional vegetarian soup stocks known to man. So say Deborah Madison and Edward Espe Brown, authors of *The Greens Cookbook*. "They are a wonderfully strong green herb with great nutritional value," the authors declare of this vitamin-C-plus-iron jackpot. Although nettles should *never* be eaten raw, once added to boiled water, they lose their sting and release what they have been guarding so fiercely: chlorophyll in abundance. The resulting broth, write Madison and Brown, "is rich, smooth, and an astounding shade of green." They point out that "soups made from the broth of boiled nettles have been known to support the lives of at least two saints—the Irish Saint Columba and the Tibetan, Milarepa." Nettle soup has long been a popular dish in Tuscany, where it is also used in *sformato,* a kind of soufflé.

This isn't to say that you should turn the wilder parts of your garden into an experimental pantry. Not every plant takes kindly to being eaten. Socrates, you'll recall, never did ask for a second cup of that hemlock. *Some plants are downright deadly, so don't eat anything until you know exactly what it is and whether or not it's safe to do so.* But do get yourself some reliable herbals and field guides and seek advice from your local gardening groups. What you learn could greatly expand your garden.

☙

In my own garden, weedology has become an important part of my apprenticeship. Finding guides is easy. Books devoted exclusively to weeds may occupy several shelves at your local library or bookshop and range from analytical tomes to chatty reports of close encounters. My favorite by far is Audrey Wynne Hatfield's decidedly upbeat *How to Enjoy Your Weeds.* Under the lively tutelage of Hatfield, who seems rarely to have met a weed whose virtues she could not discover, I have made friends with several of these plants.

Scarlet pimpernel is one such favorite. Both bold and shy, this weed closes up its miniature, salmon-red, roselike flowers by noon to hide out for the rest of the day. It's easy to see why author Baroness Orczy referred to her hero as that "damned elusive Pimpernel," for the mild-mannered Sir Percy Blakeney had a habit of appearing boldly all over the place, only to hide in plain sight upon the arrival of his enemies. The presence of this little plant tells me which areas of my soil are acidic or in need of lime.

I also like storksbill, which looks just as you'd expect, and with which you can charm even the coolest kids by showing them how to make the flower heads into scissors.

Come to think of it, how many kids today know the old game of holding a reflective buttercup under the chin to see who likes butter? Or have learned to make a daisy chain? Or have made a wish on a dandelion puffball? "Go out and play in the weeds" sounds less than inviting. Yet a lot of grown-up gardeners once found a world of imagination with weeds that today's kids can't find with a two-thousand-dollar computer.

Many plants of pedigree are little more than weeds with a few airs and graces bred into their tough little bodies. So says Mea Allan, who describes her own love-hate relationship with the weeds of England in *Weeds: The Unbidden Guests in Our Gardens*. According to Allan, the pansy, that snooty show-off with the velvety petals, is a direct descendant of "weedy little heartsease." It seems that in 1810, a noblewoman took a fancy to the ignoble weed and began transplanting different types of violas from the wild into the garden proper. The head gardener, a famous nurseryman, and several others got in on the act, crossing one weed with another until they had achieved the elegant varieties so familiar to us now.

Even the invasives carry a history worth learning if you are truly to understand the workings of your garden. Dandelions, for instance, made their way from Eurasia to various parts of Europe and most likely came to this country with the English Pilgrims, who also brought us such plants as chickweed, shepherd's purse, and plantain. The last became known by indigenous peoples as "whiteman's foot," since this invasive sprang up wherever its human counterpart walked.

Some otherwise undesirable plants have evocative names, a sufficient raison d'être to aficionados of the art of word collecting. Besides, which do you suppose is likelier to create interest, telling people you've been out pulling weeds all day or proudly declaring that you have contended, like Jacob wrestling the angel, with the mighty forces of spurge, oxalis, dogbane, nimble Will, and trailing torment? I thought so.

Whatever you do about weeds, don't just "soak 'em and choke 'em." Chemical toxins deplete the soil more than any plant can. If you must give them the old heave-ho, check out organic methods first. Or get one of those long snake-tongued trowels and meditate on your own metaphorical weeds as you reestablish order with patience. Better a small patch peacefully winnowed than a whole field shocked into submission.

Weeds, benign or otherwise, are a gardener's link with the wild. They remind us who or what is really in control here, for as the Roman poet Horace quipped some two thousand years ago, "You may drive out nature with a pitchfork, yet she'll be constantly running back."

How can we help but have respect for weeds? This seemingly ragtag bunch includes travelers, natives, historians, healers, garden helpers, beauties, toy makers, and comedians. Just as our own human quirks and foibles may contain the seeds of our greatest gifts, so too the weeds in your garden may offer resources you never knew existed.

You may even discover that a good weed is a terrible thing to waste.

The delicate first moment of dawn, before its mystery
is invaded by the clutter of daily living.

—*Virginia Gildersleeve,*
Many a Good Crusade

STRAWBERRIES
AT DAWN

The first pale amber rays of sun have backlit the somber
mountains. A coastal live oak rustles. The birds are stirring. In
my garden, the poppies are rolled up tightly like saffron
scrolls. I'm on my knees, coffee within easy reach, as I set a
blue salvia into the ground the way a parent might ease a
sleepy child back into bed.

Dawn is the best time of day to do almost anything. The

phone holds its tongue and there are no appointments. One's mind is fertile with dreams whose meanings flower best in a hushed world.

Morning people are often believed to spring out of bed alert as watchdogs, ready to race headlong into the day. The reality is not nearly so perky.

I've discovered that no matter what hour I rise, I still come into consciousness like a large ice mass beginning to thaw. Whether nearly noon or barely dawn, the transition to consciousness is slow and subtle. It's just as well to start the process when the earth is in a sympathetic mood.

So I write and garden when morning is just around the corner.

The inner critic, I've noticed, likes to sleep in, but the muse keeps odd hours and usually has quite a few things to tell me before the sun comes up. Not that I get them all down accurately, but the fragments, threads, and even mishearings I transcribe in the early hours are somehow worth more than the most sensible pronouncements of the critic later. I need them both, of course, but letting the muse speak first seems more politic.

Something similar takes place with early morning gardening. It's not that I rush out, pitchfork in hand, poised to tear into hardpan or to divide those unsuspecting clumps of daisies. Instead, I gravitate to this corner or that and slowly become aware of what the garden wishes to tell me. If the muse is not in nature, where is she?

What I accomplish at this hour, as the earth sails steadily into the light, matters not nearly as much as the way I go about it. This is a meditative time, whether I am planting tulip bulbs and raking the pathways or just hand-picking the ubiquitous snails.

It is a creative time as well. The wealth of garden and nature poetry owes much, I believe, to all the mornings when writers touched ideas in the soil that had temporarily eluded them at the keyboard or notebook. The link between tilling the land and cultivating the language has been affirmed time and time again. In the poem "Digging," Nobel Laureate Seamus Heaney describes sitting at a desk by the window in his boyhood home in Ireland. The pen rests in his hand while he listens to the rasp of his father's spade sinking into the gravelly ground, and he muses on all the generations who furrowed the land before his father. But lacking a spade—or, rather, the calling to it—how will Heaney carry on the tradition of stewarding life from that stony soil? With the clean sound of his father's spade still ringing like a bell, Heaney sees his pen in a new light. He will dig with that, patiently tilling the blank page into furrows of words ripe with significance.

In the garden, time itself seems to expand. Later in the day I may fret about getting to this appointment or achieving that task "on time," but early in the morning I seem to have all the time in the world. The killing frost of anxiety is held at bay, letting ideas and insights establish strong roots.

It is a time of solitude, which is in itself an undervalued yet precious resource. Rising at such an hour, you need not be anything particular for anybody. Just being is enough, period. The trees don't care if your hair is combed, and your status means nothing to the statice flowers. Your self-regard dissolves like dew on blue-eyed grass under the sun's first warming rays. Animal awareness takes over, and instead of mentally processing the names of things, you savor their feel and smell and sound.

Details pierce like needles pulling threads through a great tapestry. The nag of a scrub jay, the dewdrop sliding like a tear along the jasmine vine, the sweetness of oak-leaf rot—each clarifies and unifies elements of nature's art.

To garden in such solitude is hardly to work in isolation. If it's true that the early hours are inherently creative, tuned in to the daily re-creation of the world, it's also true that many souls are quietly stoking those creative fires. As I write or plant, I know that somewhere others are doing the same or else setting up an easel, walking the dog along a quiet road, doing whatever brings them and the earth into communion. Those still in bed are dreaming now, and I sense the energy of it emanating like silent waves that vibrate the roots deep underground.

Gardening early in the morning, one dispenses with goals. You could stumble out to a bench and stare at the trees as you slowly come to, and much would happen within that simple act.

It's always a good day, too, even on "bad" days, because that first vital connection has been honored. No matter how busy one gets later on, there is an abiding sense of having engaged, however briefly, in what is essential.

I didn't always live like this. Once, I viewed morning as a daily assault signaled by the buzz of the alarm. To soften the shock of seeing my face in the bathroom mirror, I relied on the caffeinated quips of TV news personalities. Kept at bay from my own thoughts by news on the car radio, I would race to the office and then launch right into water-cooler talk with colleagues. I slept later in those days but was always tired, and the thought of waking even earlier would have seemed absurd.

What I didn't yet realize was that I was living absurdly, starting each day as one might switch on a scheduled sitcom. Nothing was gradual or quiet or open to discovery. I don't miss those mornings, or the dissatisfaction that always caught up with me by evening.

Yes, it's true: I go to bed earlier than some. How I used to tease my mom, a 5 A.M. riser who liked to retreat with a good book by eight o'clock—until I discovered for myself the richness of experience that led her to plant strawberries at dawn. Now I follow the natural clock of the earth. It feels good.

As I write this, the young sunlight is causing bare patches in my garden to gleam like unwritten pages. I wonder what the story is today. And if there are any plump red strawberries just waiting to be savored.

No season, of course, is complete in itself. And our arbitrary boundaries of time are more convenient than conclusive. Summer ends and Autumn comes over the land on schedules governed by the land itself, not by either stars or calendars.

—*Hal Borland,*
Sundial of the Seasons

SUMMER'S NEARLY OVER WHEN YOU SEE THE NAKED LADIES

Stop me if you've heard this one: California has no seasons.

Living in California, I hear it often, and in all kinds of weather. Generally, the speaker adopts the tone of one who has, for years, been collecting empirical data on the subject and is now ready to go public with his or her brilliant conclusion.

I have been privy to the no-season theory on days when the dappling sun of spring releases the scent of rain-wet sage, and the plum trees turn pink and white with blossom. I have heard it when the autumn fields are rich in seed and the evening primroses, having come into their own at last, glow like lanterns in the harvest sunset. I have heard it even as snow gentled the look and toughened the nature of nearby mountaintops. Hardly a season goes by without a visitor — or, worse, a native — informing me that there are no seasons here.

One hears similar judgments rendered on other locales as well. It always rains in Ireland. It's always hot in Arizona. And so on. There's just one problem with these mono-season appraisals. They aren't true.

Arizona, for example, boasts all but one of the world's seven main climate areas, and each of those regions and micro-regions offers a detailed roster of seasons. Autumn visitors to one of Arizona's subalpine meadows are more likely to need a warm jacket than a tube of sunblock, and gold quaking aspens, not saguaro cacti, will line their horizon.

As for Ireland, while this astoundingly green land may conjure up visions of constant showers, my actual experience includes balmy summer days when the sun hung in the sky until ten or eleven o'clock at night.

❦

How do such glib meteorological assessments take hold? One possibility is that we have come to rely less on our senses and more on simplistic reports and visual cues to determine what is and is not a bona fide season.

Take Christmas cards. No matter where you live, the card shop at the mall is more likely to abound in generic snowy images à la Currier and Ives than in depictions of your actual ecoregion as it appears in December. Thus, winter equals snow, and a narrowly specified kind of snow at that. Muddy slushes and full blizzards would hardly do.

Nor would it be cricket, so to speak, to show magnified views of snowy lands, for this would reveal the presence of thousands of snow fleas, flightless scorpion flies, and wingless snow flies. Yet according to Roger Swain, author, gardener, and biologist, such creatures are part and parcel of the winter wonderland. In his stereotype-blasting essay "White Life," Swain reports, "The most impressive invertebrate found in the snow is the snow worm. On snowfields and glaciers in California, Oregon, Washington, and Alaska, these inch-long black worms have been seen massed over more than forty acres of snow. . . . Some of them are consumed by birds; some find their way into drinks served in Yukon bars."

Not that I think any the less of snow. Although I meet it only occasionally here in California, during my childhood years snow and I were, you might say, closer than most. One winter day when I was three years old and my family, who would soon move to California, still lived on Narcissus Drive in Syosset, New York, I went outside, as usual, to play in the snow. This meant, of course, that my busy mother first had to spend the better part of an hour guiding my hyperactive body into several layers of underclothes and woolens, followed by a full-length red snowsuit, the fit and look of which was not unlike sausage casing.

When I ran, or rather trundled, off into the garden, I like to think that she curled up with one of her beloved books, but it's more likely that she immediately moved on to the next task at hand. At any rate, a few moments passed.

Returning to the kitchen, my mother's eye was caught by a pile of familiar red fabric. It was the snowsuit, which lay in a heap under the table. Then she saw the sweater. And the long pants. And the thermal underwear. Following the trail of clothing out the back door and into the garden, what should she see but thirty pounds of curly-headed trouble perched on top of the redwood fence, singing out loud and clear. Not a stitch on me, and the snow falling in great billowy puffs.

"Joyce, dear," she said, "what are you doing?" She was a very patient woman.

According to my mother, I looked at her as if I'd never heard such a superfluous question in all my life. What did it *look* like I was doing?

"I'm singing to the snowflakes," I replied. Couldn't she see that?

Yes, I have been one acquainted with the snow.

❦

In those regions where snow—romantic, wormy, or otherwise—is not delivered, winter nonetheless arrives. In much of the Pacific Northwest, winter is lush, green, and wet, while in New Orleans the Christmas lights get competition from the vibrant hibiscus. In many parts of California, the true color of winter is not white but red, which burns like a Yule flame in hedges of pyracantha, mounds of poinsettia, and the bright red berries of native holly and laurel trees. As my friend Maude Meehan writes in "Corcoran Lagoon," "The seasons here / pass gently, announced by / certain flowering / or a subtle change of light."

Still the stereotypes proliferate. The calendars with snowy winter scenes flip, in June, to images of tanned swimmers cavorting on a beach. But if you lived in Sydney, Australia, you would be getting your skis and woolies out of storage at about this time. Some will argue that the seasons south of the equator are "reversed," an intriguing notion in itself, since it implies that everything north of the equator is "right" and everything south is "wrong." Yet even in so-called sunny California, June tends to come clothed in morning fog, and the average temper-

ature here on the central coast is a mild 58 degrees. So
strapped are we to the idea of summer as three solid months of
sun that every year Californians puzzle over this seemingly
aberrant phenomenon.

Rain in California throws a lot of people off, too. We're
surprised when it happens, worried when it doesn't, and tend
to forget that it's part of a greater pattern. When John Stein-
beck set *East of Eden* in Monterey County's great Salinas Valley, he noted, "The water came in a thirty-year cycle. . . . And
it never failed that during the dry years the people forgot about
the rich years, and during the wet years they lost all memory of
the dry years."

My forty-year-old Webster's dictionary defines *season* as
"any one of the four arbitrary periods into which the year is divided." *Arbitrary* is the key word. What we have come to think
of as a typical day in spring, summer, autumn, or winter has
more to do with our own narrow constructs than with observations of nature in its actual shifting complexity. Seasons
exist, all right, but they manifest in ways as varied as moment
is from moment. They are rich in nuance, subtle in transition.
Yet, for the most part, we treat seasons as if they clicked over
like digits on an analog clock.

Reinforcing this rigidity is our evolution into *Homo Interior.*
We spend so much of our time indoors that it has spawned ab-
surdities we have come to consider normal. Such as driving ten
miles to walk around an indoor track. Throwing wet laundry
into electric dryers on warm, windy days. Buying artificial

flowers at a crafts store whose construction kills off a natural meadow. Checking the weather on TV more often than we stop to gaze up at the sky.

Between climate control and Madison Avenue, it's no wonder that many people consider it a change of seasons when local merchandisers replace the back-to-school wares they've been hawking all summer with the Christmas cards of late August.

Stores also provide us, whenever we want, with fresh produce that nature would have us wait for. You want cantaloupe in January? You got it. Strawberries in March? No problem. Most shoppers expect to find tomatoes year-round. Of course, they won't be *ripe* tomatoes, but they will be uniformly red, round, and the size of tennis balls, whose taste they are likely to resemble. Such are the trade-offs. To taste authentically prime fruits and vegetables, barring preserves, one needs to believe in seasons and to develop a calendar of the palate.

Cut off from the source, we miss out on the true richness of seasons, forgetting how diverse and subtle and localized each one can be. We stop using our senses until whatever we are told—or, rather, sold—about the world seems true.

The remedy is to become observant of what we ourselves experience, familiarizing our very bones with the dynamic patterns of change.

Which brings me to the naked ladies. Also known as *Amaryllis belladonna* or *Brunsvigia rosea,* they are wild lilies, whose luridly pink blossoms seem to pop out of nowhere at

❦

summer's end. Here on the central coast the naked ladies pa-
rade along roadsides, surprise you en masse in ditches, and
race gleefully among the foothills. Until this, their one sensa-
tional moment, they have been enclosed in leafless stalks that
resemble charred rhubarb. Who would guess that those unpromising sticks were magic wands, ready to conjure up a
bevy of burlesque beauties? The naked ladies are summer's
last fling, a cartoon-colored reminder to hit the beaches, take a
day off, go have some fun. For pretty soon it will be time—if
only by the calendar—for stocking the firewood, making sure
the tires can handle rain-slicked roads, and other serious-
minded stuff.

❦

Time was when diarists kept ongoing accounts of changes in
season and the land. Among the most famous journals is Edith
Holden's handwritten and vividly illustrated daybook, *The
Country Diary of an Edwardian Lady.* Her daily observations
counter stereotypical views of the seasons. For example, in
mid-autumn of 1906, she notes, "Scarcely any of the trees [in
Warwickshire] is turned colour. . . . Weather still continues
perfect. Hot sun during the day, cold and clear at night, mist in
the mornings."

In a fall commentary written a century earlier, Jane
Austen complains about the heat: "What dreadful weather we
have! It keeps me in a continual state of inelegance." So much

for typical English weather—rain all day, fog all night, and the autumn leaves turning red and gold in time for tea.

A diarist closer to home was Hal Borland, legendary outdoor editorial writer for *The New York Times* who died in 1978. *Sundial of the Seasons*, first published in 1943 and now sadly out of print, brought together 365 short essays, one for each day of the year, beginning with the vernal equinox.

A keen observer of the world outdoors, Borland knew that real seasons do not fit into neat little boxes. "February," he noted, "is a gardener pruning his grapevines today and shoveling a two-foot drift off the front walk tomorrow." Later in the year he remarked, "Summer comes not by the calendar any more than snow waits for a definite date in December." His nature journal is a testament to daily attention, by which one little detail can become the seed that blossoms into a rich harvest of insight.

Keeping a garden journal is as open to possibilities as gardening itself. There is no one way to do it. It can bloom along the margins of an existing journal or appointment book. It can command a place of its own, trellising sentences like sweet peas along the blue lines of a note pad or spreading out in all directions on the virgin ground of a blank book. Like a patio plant, it can even flourish in containers such as index cards filed away with pretty seed packets.

The nature of the gardening journal may reflect—or counterbalance—the personality of the gardener. It may be practical and organized as a vegetable garden or daydreamy and

101

SUMMER'S
NEARLY OVER
WHEN YOU SEE
THE NAKED
LADIES

rambling as wildflowers in a field. Like a potting shed, it gives beauty and composition to the oddest assortment of garden miscellany—sketches, recipes, pressed flowers, addresses of nurseries, photos of your grandmother's Lincoln roses.

Like both garden and gardener, it evolves, moving from the determined to the surprised, the mundane to the poetic, the potential to the actual, and onward, ever more certainly, into uncertainty.

If you would like to keep a garden journal but do not have a great deal of time, fear not. Regularity, not copious output, is the key to success. In the movie *Smoke*, a vendor makes a point of taking just one photograph every morning at the same time from the same spot in front of his store. Over years he compiles a unique and often haunting view of New York City.

Similarly, a garden journal may thrive as a series of conscious snapshots. Every day take five or ten minutes to note just one thing about the garden and one observation of the weather. My own notation for one particular day in June reads, "A goldfinch finds purchase on the bobbing cosmos flowers as easily as my feet balance on the spinning earth. Gentle sun and a mild breeze bring me the scent of grass and freshly lavendered sheets on the clothesline." Those few details awaken a host of others, bringing past into present like a winter's taste of summery fruit preserve.

This year, I'm experimenting with devoting my journals almost exclusively to the outdoor world. Whereas in years past,

I could go on for pages about a frustrating day at the office or make long lists of things to do, I've begun pruning back the verbiage to focus on the year as it might appear to nature's eye. The effect, so far, has been to put daily ups and downs into perspective and to take me out of my smaller self, not in the sense of avoiding introspection but in the sense of giving that introspection a greater range of perceptual field, moving into the greater Self that breathes with the wind, grows with all of nature, and communes with eternity even as the seasons change.

SUMMER'S
NEARLY OVER
WHEN YOU SEE
THE NAKED
LADIES

O Tiger-lily," said Alice . . . "I wish you could talk!"

"We can talk," said the Tiger-lily, "when there's any-body worth talking to."

—Lewis Carroll,
Through the Looking-Glass

IN PRAISE OF FLOWERY SPEECH

"Hey."

"Oh, hi there."

"How's it going?"

"Good. What're you up to?"

"Oh, you know. Same old same old. Keepin' busy. How's work going?"

"Okay. Real busy. Know what I mean?"

"Do I! Well, gotta run. Good talkin' to you."

"Yeah, you too. Take care."

"Take care."

Does this exchange sound at all familiar? When you run into a neighbor, colleague, or friend at the supermarket or video store you have to say *something*, right? So what do you say? Not much. A few basic salutations, the obligatory nod to how busy we all are, and—well, that's about it.

Once upon a time, or so I have been told, there was this curious custom known as conversing. Passing acquaintances would express delight at encountering the other person, inquire after each other's health and that of their family, and perform, however perfunctorily, a mutual color commentary on the weather and local scenery. They would then give each other some sort of blessing and depart, feeling much the better for having met. In some instances, one person might actually go so far as to invite the other person's family to dine with them that very week so as to prolong the pleasure of conversing, a gesture that seems all the more curious when one considers that the personal planner book was not yet de rigueur, thus obliging the inviter and the invitee simply to *make time* for one another. Amazing.

Today's exchanges tend to be much more streamlined. Gone are the spur-of-the-moment invitations, and changes in the weather and the land around us seldom rate a mention.

The busyness is a pity. If we have time to rent a video, then maybe we have time to double the pasta recipe and ask friends to join us. (Just like that? Just like that.)

The loss of the other pleasantries may not, at first blush, seem to be such a big deal. But take another look at that first exchange. Not only is it fairly typical, it is also unrelentingly dull. Even when we do liven up our speech, we tend to draw not on such sources as weather, the land, current local events, or literature, but to latch on to whatever sitcom jargon, ad slogan, or tabloid tidbit is floating around. Like TV news commentators with a few extra seconds before the commercial, we as a culture have become expert at chatting without communicating anything at all.

Of all the language sources, the loss of nature seems the saddest. A thousand times a day, nature—in the most ordinary of places—has something to tell or show us; something it wants us to touch, smell, or feel; something it wants all of us, not just the overtly artistic, to express.

"What's new?" someone says.

"Nothing," we reply. But on that very day, golden poppies have burst out all over the hills. Did we see them?

"Whaddya hear?" someone asks.

"Not much," we say. But the meadowlark sings for free,

and at night the wind howls as we lie snug in our beds. Do we listen?

Our everyday speech reflects our separation from nature. Rushed through checkout lines with barely enough time to write out the check, we may mutter, "Have a good one," but who exchanges friendly comments about the weather? When we do mention the weather, too often we're reporting an item we saw on TV rather than a phenomenon we observed while outside.

Even when talking about place, we may leave nature out of it. Describing where we live, we're more inclined to mention freeway exits and malls than landforms and vegetation. This is partly because the names of subdivisions and overdeveloped towns have become meaningless. Sycamore Ridge may be flat and treeless, while Brookhaven may no longer offer either the flow of water or anything remotely resembling a paradisical wilderness.

Yet nature longs to leap onto the tongue, and the more we speak that living language, the more present and powerful nature becomes. Here, then, are some ideas for fertilizing the garden of language.

- *Feed your seedlings.* To a small child, "The sun's going down now" means a lot more than "Bedtime at seven o'clock." Likewise, we need to engage children in conversations about seasonal happenings—"What a breezy March morning this is!" or "Look how red the leaves are getting"—instead of letting the merchandisers quite literally ring the changes. Be sure, too, that the books you share at bedtime include stories, poems, and songs about the land.

- *Dig deep.* Another way to reclaim the buried language of the land is through local histories. Your librarian, native gardening group, or wildlife volunteer can help you get started. First-time visitors to Elkhorn Slough, a wetlands preserve not far from my home, are often at a loss to guess how the region got its name. When they find out that elk once roamed widely there, the visitors playfully smack their foreheads and grin. But of course! The smiles give way to sadness when they learn that the extinction of the elk occurred not hundreds of years but merely decades ago, thanks to a single hunting lodge. (It is now defunct. You can't shoot what doesn't exist.) Yet even in such a depressing anecdote, a seed of hope takes root. For what strikes visitors then is the wish to save the remaining wild animals and plants from the fate of becoming mere syllables with no living referent.

- *Name the place.* You might consider adopting the Irish tradition of naming one's home, a powerful way to invoke the spirit of place. You can do this whether you live in a rambling house or a cozy apartment. My son's grandparents in Galway call their house *Ríona,* Gaelic for *heart,* a name that perfectly sums up the warmth of welcome there. Your chosen name might tie into something that thrives in your garden or local area, as in Morning-glory Corner, Bluejay Studio, or Pinetree Place.

- *Broadcast seeds among the rows.* Not sure how to begin your letters to friends and family? Make a point of telling about some change, however subtle, in the garden. Or describe your current impressions of the area around you. A letter I sent home from New Mexico began, "The cottonwoods are in their golden glory now. We had the first snowfall of the season yesterday, but the sun took one look at the lacy white trees and decided it missed the color. So by late afternoon we were back to bright blue windowsills, displays of red chile *ristras*, terra-cotta tiles, and leaves like golden coins, capped off by a sky turning royal purple." "What's new?" isn't limited to what you are doing. Indeed, the biggest news of all may be what you are *noticing*.

- *Love a rose by any other name.* Commit to learning the names of five native wildflowers this year. Find out the name of those trees that line your favorite street downtown. What kind of birds frequent those trees? You can also use a book like *Flowers and Their Histories* by Alice M. Coats to discover fascinating stories behind even the commonest flowers in your garden. Other ideas? Search resources about Native America to learn the many different names given to each full moon in the lunar calendar. Once a month ask a different family member to find out how that month got its name.

- *Come to your senses.* Once, I skimmed the descriptive parts of novels. Now I savor them. After all, who would want to rush through the following passage, a summation of the elements of happiness, from the American classic *My Ántonia* by Willa Cather?

I sat down in the middle of the garden, where snakes could scarcely approach unseen, and leaned my back against a warm yellow pumpkin. There were some ground-cherry bushes growing along the furrows, full of fruit. I turned back the papery triangular sheaths that protected the berries and ate a few. All about me giant grasshoppers, twice as big as any I had ever seen, were doing acrobatic feats among the dried vines. The gophers scurried up and down the ploughed ground. There in the sheltered draw-bottom the wind did not blow very hard, but I could hear it singing its humming tune up on the level, and I could see the tall grasses wave. The earth was warm under me, and warm as I crumbled it through my fingers.

- *Store a little of the harvest.* If you keep a gardening journal or scrapbook, use it to collect poems and quotations about nature and gardening. Invite your family to fill the kitchen calendar with brief observations about the season. Don't worry about waxing poetic. Just start off with such jottings as "Cold today!" and "Bright green dragonfly." Then watch what develops as the months unfold and perceptions sharpen.

• *Fertilize the common ground.* You may be pleasantly surprised at what develops when you invite nature back into casual conversations. Once at the grocery store I mentioned that the heavy rains were turning the hills as green as Ireland. "Funny you should mention that," said the clerk. It turned out she was planning her first trip to Ireland but couldn't decide on an itinerary. The next time I went in, I dropped off some notes and old brochures.

On another occasion, my friend Karen admired a gorgeous wreath of dried flowers on the wall of her dentist's otherwise sterile office. "I made that," the receptionist said proudly, and after they had talked a little longer, she invited Karen to stop at her garden on the way home and help herself to some lavender and statice. Soon, these people, who had barely exchanged more than a sentence in five years, were trading flower seeds and gardening tips whenever they met.

• *Return to the source.* We check our e-mail. We check the answering machine. We skim the newspaper while we watch TV. Maybe that's enough for the brain, but the heart wants more. And less. When was the last time you simply sat in the garden, or on your balcony, or at the local park? Took a silent walk around the block with someone you love? Lay on your back on a grassy hill looking up at the clouds? It sounds corny only because so many of us have forgotten how tremendous it feels to be filled up with the silent wisdom and ordinary eloquence of nature.

Autumn

HONORING

THE

HARVEST

*E*verything that slows us down and forces patience, everything that sets us back into the slow circles of nature, is a help. Gardening is an instrument of grace.

—*May Sarton,*
Journals

CYCLES AND SCHEDULES

My friends Amber and Bernard are coming to dinner next week. Amber and I have jostled our schedules around to make it work. Armed with only a pencil and an appointment book, I alter the tenor of days to suit myself. Cancel this, reschedule that, change P.M. to A.M. I'm taking control of "my" time.

Later I put together a mental menu of fresh vegetables from the garden. I want this dinner to reflect how special

Amber and Bernard are to us. The potatoes are ready and there is plenty of lettuce. Then I look out the kitchen window, glaring at the tall green cornstalks. "If only I'd known," I say, "I would have planted you ten days sooner." As I deep-water the patch, I urge it, only half joking, to "hurry up, grow faster."

People have schedules. Plants have cycles.

People will stay up late, get up early, skip meals, cut corners, drive too fast, and otherwise work themselves into a frenzy to get something done in less time. Some people live their entire lives this way, rushing from one thing to the next, perpetually poised to seize the future.

Plants aren't like that. Oh, sure, you can root-prune a tomato plant to trick the fruit into ripening sooner. You can soak seeds overnight to hasten sprouting. And no doubt the geneticists are fooling around with the timing of food crops along with everything else. But that's all about human intervention. Left to itself, a plant will take every day, every moment that it requires. Plants know just what is meant by "the fullness of time," a phrase that seems to have slipped from our revved-up cut-to-the-chase conversations.

One of the most important yet least mentioned aspects of gardening is waiting. There is nothing passive about this waiting, either. The word *wait* comes from the same ancient Indo-European base for words like *wake* and *watch* and meant, at one time, to secretly keep an eye out for something or someone. In gardening, this translates into patient and daily attentiveness, taking the time to consider what is happening in the garden right now and to see within it the seeds of what will come. So all alone one morning, still in your bathrobe, you may stroll between the raised beds to see if any sprouts are beginning to push through the soil. There may be something for you to do: evict a snail, water the soil. Or there may be nothing you *can* do right now—other than to show up and notice what is happening all around you. To trust that nature is steadily working away and need not be forced, such as by chemical fertilizers. To respect nature. To wait.

A small town in Ireland once taught me a lesson in tempering one's endless expectations. As a child, I had holidayed in Kilfinane with my parents and siblings. One day, my mother sent three of us children to the corner shop to pick up the newspaper, some cream, and a head of lettuce. When we came back a good while later empty-handed, Mom asked us if we had forgotten our errand. No, we said, and told her what the shopkeeper had told us: "The newspaper will be in at half-past four. The cream will be in on Tuesday. And the lettuce will arrive in May." That's the kind of story that could get me in trouble with friends in Ireland, where you can now get anything at any time in vast and ultramodern emporia, yet I quite cherish the memory. Sure, didn't we manage just grand, cooling our heels a wee bit?

Close cousin to waiting is preparation.

When I plant vegetables, I know that as a rule it will take

about twelve weeks from germination to harvest. In other words, a season. The lettuce seeds that I sow in the early morning chill of late autumn will surface as green, ruffled harbingers of the coming spring.

Even before the sowing date comes, however, I will have prepared the raised bed to take the seeds. This means working in compost, the rich dark substance that results from the gradual breakdown of organic materials.

Compost happens, as they say, but this too will have taken time. Food that might otherwise have been wasted is returned to the earth with other suitable materials, ranging from dryer lint and garden clippings to eggshells and chicken manure. Over days, weeks, and months the materials will have broken down, becoming the crumbly nutrient-rich substance known as *brown gold*.

Yet even before working in the compost, I may have planted a cover crop, replenishing the soil from a previous crop of heavy-feeding vegetables. That means giving the rye grass, alfalfa, or clover a good six weeks or more to fill the raised bed with a thick layer of green. Add another day to turn the crop under into the soil. A few more days to let it start breaking down.

Before any of *this* can happen, Jerry will have built the raised bed, carefully salvaging, measuring, cutting, setting up, and hammering the wood. Wood from a tree that, long before Jerry and I were born, was slowly and steadily sending its roots into the nourishing soil. Soil that had built up over centuries.

By the time that lettuce reaches the plate it will have completed a cycle that pretty well encapsulates the formation of the earth. There's truth to the jest of scientist Carl Sagan, who said, "If you want to make an apple pie from scratch, you must first create the universe."

❦

I stop and consider this on the day that my waiting for the corn to grow has turned into impatience. Impatience is a break in the natural cycle, an absurd insistence that things be other than they are. Acts of impatience more often squelch possibilities than promote them. Think of the old children's story of the farmer who tries to help the carrots grow by tugging at them and ends up with a handful of spindly roots and no garden at all. My own impatience has "achieved" similar results in both the literal and metaphoric gardens of my life, while those aspects of my life that flourish owe much to learning how to prepare and to wait.

So it is as well today to let go of my impatience. Instead, I think about how far corn has traveled and how much it has gone through in order to become this green and ripening crop in my backyard.

About five thousand years ago in Central and South America, farmers tended a certain wild grass, at the top of which grew a single small pod of corn. The pod looked nothing like the long, evenly toothed ears one sees at the market today. Fertilized by another grass called teosinte, and perhaps by the pollen of other plants, pod corn continued to evolve. Over the next several hundred years it became hardier and the ears lengthened to hold more kernels.

The practice of growing corn spread north. By the time the first European settlers arrived in North America, the indigenous peoples had virtually perfected the art of growing, storing, and using corn, as well as incorporating it into their spiritual rites and festivals. Corn has been here far longer than most of our ancestors have.

Once more I look at the green cornstalks. Wind sings through them as if through a harp. In that rustling sound I hear the story of ancient beginnings, rich ancestry, and an approach to life that is grounded in the sacred.

I decide to practice the lost art of waiting.

During my first twelve years of school, I figure that my teachers offered a total of less than six uninterrupted hours in the marvelous natural laboratory at our doorstep: the Indiana Dunes. . . . Even in a place so well suited for nature study, my teachers kept us inside classrooms a thousand hours for every one hour they took us into the field.

—Gary Paul Nabhan
in The Geography of Childhood

FEEDING THE ROOTS OF CHILDHOOD

It's a beautiful day in the neighborhood, a warm bright September afternoon. A group of elementary and middle-school students walks home from the school bus stop. As usual, they have first stopped at a local fast-food establishment. Not that there is anything distinctly local about it, since there are millions more just like it all over the world. The children munch their burgers and sip their caffeinated soft drinks as they make their way toward empty houses and noisy TVs.

Some of the children have spent part of the day sitting in a darkened classroom watching a video about a rain forest somewhere in Central America. If pressed, they could provide you with several facts about it.

What they might not know is that there is a critical relationship between the rain forests and the hamburgers they are eating. According to Jeremy Rifkin in *Beyond Beef: The Rise and Fall of the Cattle Culture,* more than 25 percent of the forests of Central America have been cleared since 1960 to create pasturelands for cattle, whose beef is imported by the United States at the rate of *several hundred thousand tons* per year. Based on Rifkin's evidence, each quarter-pound hamburger eaten by these kids may have cost the destruction of 165 pounds of living matter, including a staggering number of plant, insect, bird, mammal, and reptile species.

Here's another intriguing connection. The students, whose homework tonight includes finding out more about the rain forest, are themselves walking through a forest. At least they are walking through what is left of one. On either side of the pavement that curves toward the subdivision, a dense forest and its undergrowth fills the air with the scents of pine, sage, and oak.

Like the rain forest, this local forest is under threat. Houses and an extravagant number of malls have encroached upon the area. A freeway bypass is under consideration. Cars greatly outnumber pedestrians and native animals. The children know—even if the few remaining animals do not—that resident drivers rarely obey the 25-mile-per-hour speed limit but take the blind narrow-shouldered curves as fast as they can.

But were you to ask the children to describe this environment—to name its common plants and animals and to tell you a little of its history—they would look at you blankly. The *rain forest* is an environment. This is just some boring place they see every day. They pass by it. They do not explore it. Indeed, the younger children, many of whom are still curious about it, have been cautioned that wooded areas are inherently dangerous, places where shadowy predators might lurk. They know never to walk through the forest alone. Nor have they gone for walks there with Mom and Dad.

Just before the forest gives way to the subdivision, the children get rid of their fast-food wrappers, cups, boxes, and bags. Some simply scatter the trash along the roadside, where a passing driver has already deposited a mound of cigarette butts. Others turn the process into a game, balling up the brightly dyed papers and pitching them as far as possible into the weeds. Those "weeds" include many native herbs, grasses, and unusual flowers, including a Douglas iris that tends to hide its deep purple among thick undergrowth. The kids don't know the names of any of these plants, but then again, most of their overworked parents and teachers don't know them either.

At home, the TV, the CD player, computer games, and the telephone await. A sunny autumn day is no competition, and besides, the kids have already had recess on the asphalt playground at school.

Some kids go straight to their homework, if only to get it over with. Use Diagram A to label the parts of a flower. [It isn't any particular flower, just a flower.] . . . Write two or three paragraphs about life in Colonial Williamsburg. . . . Solve this problem: If a farmer lost 17% of her alfalfa and 9% of her root vegetables, what fraction of her total crop did she lose? . . . List five causes of pollution.

When one or both parents come home, the TV gets switched over to the news. The family may or may not eat together, depending on everyone's schedule and degree of tiredness. At any rate, dinner is less likely to come from the backyard or a local farmer's market than from the convenience aisle of a major grocery chain. Or—as a "treat" that has become more and more the norm—the family may pile into the car and go out for fast food. As they drive along, nobody speaks. The car radio is on, private reverie has given way to individual distraction, and the surrounding area is so familiar it has become invisible.

🌱

What's wrong with this picture? Everything. In our culture, direct contact with nature has become an endangered species all its own.

But children need nature. They need to stain their faces purple by eating plums picked from an actual tree. To wiggle bare toes in cool mud as they watch water striders crossing the surface of a stream. To explore meadows with the family and to learn the name of a grandparent's favorite local flower. To plant a tree and measure its growth by theirs. To know what kind of bird sings outside their kitchen window. Only then will lessons about the rain forest, migrating whales, and any other aspect of the environment take root.

So often we talk about learning in terms of preparing our children "to face the real world." (How revealing that we express it in terms of confrontation rather than relationship.) But what exactly do we mean by the *real* world? Is it the high-speed world of business, the abstract world of the intellect, the shallow world depicted on TV, the mirror world of social pressure and expectation? Or is it a living, breathing world in which, as the naturalist John Muir observed, everything is connected with everything else? If it is this last, our children are ready for it right now and need only their sense of wonder, the guardianship of an elder, and a little unstructured time to start their lifelong apprenticeship.

My son Eoghan (pronounced Owen) once said to me, "When I grow up, the smell of sage will bring my childhood back to me." This is my hope: that his childhood will come back in the sights and scents of rolling hills covered in manzanita, oak trees, and sage and dotted with flowers like coast prettyface, yellow lupine, and wild yarrow. That it will look like red-tailed hawks, mule deer, and the rare gray fox. That it will sound like owls, crickets, and frogs chorusing at night and the grinding song of a ruby-throated hummingbird by day. That it will dance again in memory like a swirling cloud of tiny junco finches and monarch butterflies. That it will feel like a handful of loamy sweet soil and taste like honeysuckle and midsummer tomatoes.

You can't buy that at the store or heat it up in the microwave, no matter what pastoral image graces the label. You can't even get it by watching the occasional nature program. Indeed, you could learn more about nature, in my opinion, by studying a square foot of soil around a suburban tree for half an hour than by spending the same amount of time in front of the Discovery Channel. Nor can you get it "on automatic," letting nature function as an increasingly diminished backdrop to the main action. At some point, you need to notice that you yourself are a part of nature and then respond, simply and daily, to that amazing revelation.

Author and Jungian analyst Marion Woodman once wrote that our contemporary culture is not just sleep-deprived but consequently dream-deprived, with a resultant cost to our imagination and development. When children lack an intimate relationship with nature, their sensory perceptiveness measurably decreases and so too, I think, does their compassion, responsibility, and patience—all those qualities that signify awareness of sharing the world with others. They also miss out on joy—on the invaluable capacity to derive and transmit great pleasure from the simplest things — not to mention gratitude. After all, the very trees are working to help them breathe, but to read this in a textbook is not at all the same as knowing it deep in your cells.

Thanks to the Internet, we live in an age in which it is far easier for a child to access information about nature than to experience it. Contact with common wild animals and native plants is increasingly rare. Stephen Trimble, coauthor of *The Geography of Childhood*, reveals that in a 1992 survey of North American fifth and sixth graders, "9 percent of the children said that they learned environmental information from home; 31 percent reported that they learned from school; and a majority, 53 percent, listed the media as their primary teacher."

Curiously, nature itself does not figure as a learning source. However, as Gary Paul Nabhan points out, "We need to return to learning about the land by being *on* the land or, better, by being *in* the thick of it."

Of course, we *are* in the thick of it. We've just forgotten this, and the hard pace and consumer values of our culture work against remembering.

To truly acknowledge that nature exists requires slowing down and simplifying our lives enough to literally feel the land's aliveness. This is something that every toddler intuitively knows and that most children, however unintentionally, are conditioned to forget. As the schedule of today's child more and more rivals that of the overworked adult, nature becomes compartmentalized and then forgotten. With little chance to

know and to love their local environment, to become personally aware of its needs and resources, future generations are
unlikely to effect a change in the dangerous patterns of over-
consumption. Without a grounding in the wisdom and balance
of nature, children become adults who run numbly through
episodic days, mere actors drifting through discrete two-
dimensional sets. Nature becomes Other.

But the truth is, we need to experience nature because we
are nature. To nurture this remembrance in our children is to
deepen awareness within ourselves.

Finding a way into nature does not have to be a compli-
cated endeavor. It can be as simple as turning off the television,
listening to a chorus of creekside frogs, looking out the window,
making hideaways in fields of tall grasses, planting pumpkin
seeds, taking a walk. The wilderness begins in wonder, the garden in caring. The following are just a few gardening-related
ideas to help you and the children in your life get started. May
they inspire many more.

- *Find out what grows* in your own suburban neighborhood,
  city block, or rural area. You don't need to start off with a
  field guide, although you will find yourselves consulting
  one quite readily once that sense of curiosity is awakened.
  Simply take walks and talk about what you discover. Ask
  and encourage lots of questions. "What kind of tree is the
  one we pass every morning? Those flowers on it look just
  like teacups!" The idea is not so much to acquire facts as to

sharpen attention. Bring all your senses into play. Compare the barks of trees by touch, notice the fragrance of the air in different weathers. Listen for birds and the sound of the wind. Gradually, you will become attuned to seasonal changes. As your awareness grows, you will detect changes from day to day and even hour to hour.

- *Don't have a yard? Adopt a local park or wildlife area.* Don't worry about becoming expert on every aspect. Just visit it the way you would a best friend or beloved relative. Home places aren't just at home but include those places where the heart can smile, the body relax.

- *Grow something, anything.* Younger children, for example, love spider plants because the offshoots are clearly the "babies" of the parent. Those offshoots are also the easiest thing in the world to transplant. Just pinch off a baby spider, set it in a new container of potting soil, and water. Voilà!—one spider plant becomes two, three, or as many as your windowsill can accommodate. Some kids like to make name cards for their growing family of spiders. You can tell them, too, that spider plants are true superheroes, standing up to the forces of pollution better than almost any other indoor plant.

- *Give seed packets as presents.* It's too easy to fall into the habit of sending nieces and nephews cash or gift certificates "so they can get whatever they want." But what *will* they want if no one stirs their creativity and sense of wonder? And what better way to honor a birthday than to give something that literally encapsulates the life force? There is more magic and possibility contained in one sunflower seed than in a shelfload of video games and glamour dolls. So consider substituting or at least adding seeds. Not "big" enough? Throw in some biodegradable (and lightweight) pulp pots and a simple garden manual written specifically for younger readers. Better yet, include simple directions in your own hand or, if you live nearby, offer to help plant the seeds. What grows may surprise you both. I've been sending seeds to young friends and relatives for years, to honor birthdays, an achievement or rite of passage, or the coming of spring. The response I get—enthusiastic accounts of towering sunflowers, lush wildflower carpets, and "funny-faced" beans with unforgettable names like Jacob's Cattle and Speckled Yellow Eye—assures me that kids want something beyond the ubiquitous pink and black plastic toys.

- *Give children a place—or places—in the garden.* Many books talk about giving children a corner of their own, which sounds good in theory. In practice, however, a child who is growing plants with different sun and soil requirements may require a variety of small growing spots mixed in with the existing garden. Besides which, the notion of a cordoned-off little plot may have more to do with an adult desire for neatness than with a child's more playful and explorative approach to the outdoors. In my experience, young gardeners often go for bushy or towering plants that create hiding places, fantasy lands, and other play areas. Think ornamental grasses, wildflower mini-meadows, and sunflower tepees rather than long narrow rows. Kids also love edible plants and fragrant herbs conducive to playing shop, acting out favorite stories, and the like. It's okay to put the sugar snap peas out in the front yard, and pots of lemon verbena and chocolate mint are always welcome around a fort or playhouse.

- *Invite your children to grow at least one food crop.* Start small, whether your garden is indoors or outdoors. All kids need to grow their own French fries is a medium-size planter on a balcony and a handful of seed potatoes. (Visit www.irish-eyes.com.) Or opt for a nonstop popcorn crop. (Hop over to Pinetree Garden Seeds at www.superseeds. com.) It is also incredibly transformative for children to eat something they themselves have grown. There develops a sense of helping to provide for one's family, an awareness of how food gets to the table and the factors that affect its journey, and an interest in how people feed themselves around the world. Young growers eat more fruit and vegetables, too, because home-grown produce just tastes better, and besides, they've put their own effort into growing it.

- *Forget radishes.* How many children do you know who like to *eat* radishes? Yet vegetable gardening kits for kids invariably include this fast germinator. On the other hand, a Sungold cherry tomato, whose fruits taste candy sweet, may be just the ticket. Buy it as a four-inch start for easier growing.

- *Involve your children, even when just shopping for groceries.* I'm not talking about pushing them down the long narrow aisles of some titanic grocery chain. Frankly, a lot of kids who "don't behave" in such settings are simply exhibiting a logical reaction to weird lighting, canned music, and psychedelic packaging, not to mention the cumulative effects of ingesting all the additives that go into processed foods. Instead, even if you can only find time to do it once a month, take them to a farmer's market, preferably organic, where they can touch, smell, and even taste the food as well as meet the families who grew it. Fresh air, auto-free streets, live music, and inexpensive but healthy food booths can turn the routine task of purchasing food into a rich experience.

- *Start a gardening program if your school has none.* Contact a school that has one to learn how to get started or send for *The Children's Garden,* a school garden start-up guide. (Contact author Jody Main, 227 Highland Terrace, Woodside, CA 94062. All proceeds benefit the Woodside School Garden.)

- *Plant trees together.* Whether at home or, with permission, at your local park, planting a tree is a powerful act of connection with the earth. What better way to mark a child's birthday, commemorate the passing of a beloved grandparent, or conclude the Christmas season? Moving house?

Plant a tree before you go as a kind of blessing on the land. Then plant another in the new place to establish a sense of home.

- *Take a leaf from home schoolers and move your classroom outside.* There's a world of difference between labeling the parts of a generic flower on a worksheet and trying to identify the real thing! Home-schooled kids also tend to incorporate local settings and sensory images into their writing, relate environmental sciences to actual gardens and wildlands, and adapt such abstract subject areas as math and critical thinking to hands-on situations such as figuring out the square footage of a vegetable plot or designing a tree house.

The thirteenth-century Turkish poet Rumi said, "There are hundreds of ways to kneel and kiss the earth." These ideas are just a few ways to awaken the garden of a child's heart. Whether your way into nature begins in an urban park, the local 4-H club, a tiny window box, or a vast expanse of wilderness is up to you. What matters is to plant the seed.

he word humility (also human) is derived from the Latin humus, meaning "the soil." Perhaps this is not simply because it entails stooping and returning to earthly origins, but also because, as we are rooted in this earth of everyday life, we find in it all the vitality and fertility unnoticed by people who merely tramp on across the surface, drawn by distant landscapes.

—Piero Ferrucci,
Inevitable Grace

NURSERIES VS. WORSERIES

There are nurseries, and then again there are plant warehouses. Call them worseries.

At nurseries, you can seek advice from a seasoned group of gardeners, several of whom may hold degrees in horticulture.

At worseries, you can watch as pallets of delicate flowers are slam-dunked from juggernauts onto the asphalt by plant wranglers. Move 'em in, move 'em out, seems to be the mission statement here, and I'm not just referring to the plants.

At worseries, whatever spindly overpriced plant you point to will seemingly thrive under the horticultural equivalent of crash-test conditions. And who do you suppose gets cast as the dummy?

At one discount chain where the plant warehouse exists as a kind of afterthought—something to hold down the sidewalk until the mutilated Christmas trees come along—I watched as a woman showed the employee three different kinds of corn starts she was hoping to plant together. "That's okay, isn't it?" she asked. "Yes," came the sagacious response, meaning, I suppose, that it was okay with *him*. Why should he care that corn, unlike tomatoes, cross-pollinates and mixing corn plants will produce inedible mutants that look like a bad day at the dentist?

Not that the woman had bought enough plants to make a difference. You need a nice solid block, or at least a long line, of corn to make sure that all that wafting pollen has something to land on. Besides which, each stalk produces only a few ears. I've grown corn by intensive methods in a four-by-eight-foot raised bed, so I know you don't need a lot of land. But you do need plenty of stalks and a knowledge of this heavy feeder's care, neither of which this woman was going to get from the plant wrangler in question.

"Do I need to do anything special with them?" the trusting soul inquired.

"Nah," the plant wrangler assured her. "Just stick 'em in the ground and forget about 'em. They'll grow anywhere." And he went right back to overwatering the mildew-prone verbena. (Another couple of weeks and those lush purple beauties would be straggly, discolored wretches languishing in the plant infirmary, otherwise known as the mark-down aisle.)

Now I'm not saying I intervened. Frankly, I'm the kind of person who minds her own business—that is, if I'm at home and there's nobody else around.

However, I may have mentioned that for the price of less than one of those chemically greened plants, she could purchase a packet of seeds that would provide more useful information than she was likely to get from a guy whose main gardening goal was teaching plants to swim.

What did Our Man in Verbena say, you ask? Not a word. For by now it was break time and he and another employee had removed themselves to the far end of that drugstore Eden, where they were puffing away on cigarettes. Big drifts of smoke curled lazily among the defenseless green masses yearning to breathe free.

According to Shepherd Ogden of the Cook's Garden, tobacco mosaic virus, "a scourge of the whole nightshade family," is transmitted on the hands of tobacco smokers and is not always easy to recognize. Once it gets into your garden it moves into the soil, where it can persist for years. The mottled, deformed plants will have lower yields. Just as well, since the vegetables will taste bitter anyway. And don't throw the damaged plants onto your compost heap, either. They will only infect the compost.

So much for discount tomatoes.

🌿

🌿

GARDENING
BY HEART

One of the first tip-offs to a reliable nursery is that it will be set within the context of an actual garden. As well as sections of container stock, you are likely to see one or more areas where many varieties of bioregional flowers, shrubs, and trees are flourishing in season. Taking a walk through these exhibition gardens can give you a lot of ideas about garden design, companion planting, and how much space and sunlight your new plants are likely to need. Are the plants established and spreading or have they merely been stuck into the ground shopping-center style? Does the garden include the occasional bug or weed suggestive of an organic approach? Does the garden reflect the diversity of nature?

Another tip-off is the availability of information. Forget the little plastic tags, which provide such handy hints as "likes good soil" and "water regularly." (Wait, they left out "Caution: Do not plant upside down.")

For really useful information go to nurseries where people, not plastic, provide most of the answers. Perhaps one of the first questions to ask is how a given employee got into the nursery business. The person who has been gardening most of his life or who has her certificate or degree in horticulture is

obviously better qualified to answer your queries than someone whose first encounter with gardening began when they
hired on last week. Don't be afraid to ask what they like to
grow in their own gardens at home. The answers could reveal
a kindred spirit or a non-gardener of the hey-I-just-work-here
variety.

In one nursery I know of, a prominent HELP WANTED sign
reveals that prospective nursery assistants need have no experience whatsoever. This, however, does not deter customers
from putting complete faith in the guy or gal wearing the little
straw hat and wielding the hose. After all, a person who works
in a nursery must know *something* about gardening, right?
Right—about as much as the average seventeen-year-old at a
chain hardware store knows about the relative merits of Soss
hinges versus standard hinges.

If a nursery staff is knowledgeable, not only will you be
able to ask questions, chances are they will ask you some questions too. Questions such as how much sun your garden gets
and where it gets it, what kind of soil you have, and whether or
not you are planting in open ground, raised beds, or small containers. If you aren't sure of the answers, they will suggest
ways to find out.

The flow of information will be evident in other ways too.
At one of my favorite nurseries, hand-printed signs at the end
of each row of native plants give detailed accounts of the
plant's region and heritage, history of decline and revival, its
value to health or wildlife, and its cultivation requirements. In

❦

another nursery, a copious clippings file is available to customers, and the purchase of a plant includes useful brochures, many of which are produced on-site and keyed to the local environment.

Another thing to look for is whether the nursery offers free or reasonably priced lectures and classes. If not, can they tell you where such lectures and classes are held? The nursery that deserves two green thumbs-up will be the one that can help you learn about local gardening clubs, native plant societies, exhibition gardens and arboretums, and other sources of gardening information. Ask if your nursery supports any school or community gardening programs.

Follow-up service is important too, despite the fact that frenetically busy consumers seem more and more willing to write off products that disappoint and take a gamble on the next purchase — and the next. A friend of mine insists that she has a black thumb because everything she plants "just dies." Still she shops, year after year, sinking her dollars into a promise of spring that rarely makes it past a two-week engagement. Most plants, however, don't just die. Instead, they drown or dry out, get eaten by something, succumb to fungus, or pine away in a setting that's all wrong for them. Whatever the reason, a good nursery will be able to help you diagnose and in many cases save the patient. If, on the other hand, they couldn't care less that your forty-dollar fuchsia isn't flowering, the tomato leaves are curling up, and there are hundreds of little creatures making cave dwellings in your daffodil bulbs, it's time to move on—especially if their chief remedy is to reach for the bug poison or chemical fertilizer.

Finally, an element whose significance has not been scientifically established, so far as I know, is the happiness factor. Yet I have come more and more to include it in my nursery selection process. At one nursery I no longer frequent, I always had the funny feeling of having walked in on an argument which, but for the unexpected arrival of a customer, would have erupted into a murderous brawl. Boss and crew seemed always to be exchanging dagger looks of the we'll-settle-this-later variety, and there was a whole lot of stomping, snorting, and muttering going on. Not even the presence of several stone Buddhas, Quan Yins, Virgin Marys, and a veritable host of angels, gnomes, and plaster bunnies could mitigate the gloom cast by scowling faces, ominous sighs, and the scathing comments that passed for repartee.

Now I can't prove any link between the misery of the nursery and the poor performance of its plants. Still, even the plants that flourished in my garden stirred memories of tension, ill will, and the threat of imminent blood loss, hardly the associations one longs for in a garden.

When you do find a good local nursery, support it. The best nurseries perform a vital community service by preserving the link between developed land and the natural world through education, biodiversity, and an organic approach. So skip the concrete plant-a-ramas. The best nurseries are those whose healthy roots go deep into the community.

The more one gives to others, the more one possesses of one's own.

—*Lao Tzu,*
Tao-te Ching

GIVING THE
GARDEN AWAY

Today I gave seeds to several gardening friends. I like the look of these seeds. Clustered, they resemble clumps of miniature bananas. Broken up, they lie in the palm like caterpillars, apostrophes, or tiny bracelets, each one embossed with raised dots in the ancient Celtic style.

Whatever these seeds resemble now, come next spring they will emerge from several far-flung gardens as glowing flowers of yellow and orange with mid-green paddled leaves. The name of the calendula, based on the Latin word *calends*, reflects the belief that it would bloom on the first day of each month in the calendar. It might just be true. Not a day goes by when I don't encounter those suns-on-a-stem peeking out from several corners of my garden. My gratitude to them runs deep.

All these seeds were gathered from a single plant. And that plant, one of several in the garden, began as a handful of seeds that a fellow gardener gave to me. As the poet William Blake wrote, "The thankful receiver bears a plentiful harvest."

Gardeners share. They give no-occasion bouquets, leave boxes of salad vegetables and squash on your doorstep, and send you home with cuttings of geranium.

Much of my garden is a testament to the generosity of others. The wall of pink morning glories, the arbor-embracing jasmine, and that lush carpet of native daisies—each arrived as a small but promising transplant, a gift no bigger and no less significant than the handclasp of friendship. The once-diminutive tree, now an abundant and towering pine, recalls the first Christmas that Jerry and I ever celebrated together. My stepson, for whom even one square foot of soil becomes the equivalent of a master magician's hat, gave me the calendula seeds. Their dazzling gold perfectly captures Shawn's passion for living the wide-awake life.

And just as I reconnect with my mother by tending the burgeoning collection of rosemary, I glimpse the faces—and, more importantly, the essence—of family and friends by tracing our shared histories among the patchwork quilt of wild-flowers, herbs, and trees.

One seed holds the promise of infinite gardens. If you grow only one or two plants but take the time to practice the twin arts of propagation and sharing, you are co-creating not just one garden but a boundless network of gardens.

Abundance is an integral part of nature's plan. Think of a single sunflower, sending its Jack-in-the-beanstalk stem up into the sky and beaming its great round face like a second sun on any passerby. When it droops, hundreds of seeds present themselves as a rich banquet for a variety of birds. Other seeds drop like blessings on the ground. The following summer, there may be several magnificent blooms where now one sun-flower stands alone with a boldness that speaks to us of trust.

We experience the abundance of nature when we honor it in return. In many ancient traditions, no food was eaten until a sampling of each item was set down upon the earth for the gods. It is an act of mindful gratitude worth practicing today. In that sense, taking scraps to the compost pile becomes much more than a practical task. It becomes a way of thanking the very mystery that nourishes us.

The practice of generous gardening offers a vital alterna-tive to the outdated notion of scarcity economics. During a six-month period in 1996, backyard gardeners in California who participated in a project called Plant a Row for the Hungry came up with more than twenty-six tons of surplus produce for numerous food banks throughout the San Francisco Bay Area.

Thus people who add a row to their vegetable gardens for local food banks empower themselves to solve so-called unsolvable problems.

If yours is a garden limited to inedibles, you can practice this simple alternative: Start a seed jar. The "seeds" will be coins, all or most of which might come from your gardening activities. For example, you can "plant" change from the purchase of a plant or gardening tool. If you are a member of a gardening association, invite your group to incorporate the concept of a seed jar into meetings and plant sales. I know of one group of organic gardening enthusiasts who decided to use the majority of their dues to help fertilize a fledgling community garden.

Trust the earth. The more you give your garden away, the more abundantly it will bloom.

Beware of all enterprises that require new clothes.

—*Henry David Thoreau,*
Walden

USING YOUR ONION

One spring, whenever I checked on the progress of my raised vegetable beds, I noticed that despite the protective netting we had set up, small but gluttonous delegations of insects and snails were still convening in the salad patches. Other representatives of the bug world were mingling in the potato beds, the cornfield, and so on. Only the onion bed was free of crowds.

Now you're probably way ahead of me, but weeks passed

before I was struck by a blinding revelation of the obvious: An onion a day might keep the bugs away.

I consulted Louise Riotte's excellent guide to companion plants, *Carrots Love Tomatoes*. This is a listing of plants that help each other to grow well, often by repelling insects. It confirmed my intuitive discovery. The onion family, which also includes garlic, chives, shallots, and leeks, is the block parent of the garden world. It protects just about all its neighbors, except peas and beans, from predatory insects.

During the next planting cycle, I interplanted onion and garlic sets instead of giving them their own box. Sure enough, the marauders stayed away in droves, while the soil continued to teem with more cooperative forms of life.

Often, a problem in the garden has a solution growing right next to it. Both nature and many spiritually driven farming cultures have known this for a long time. For example, the antidote to many if not most poisonous plants is often to be found in the next plant over.

If this is true for the literal garden, why not bring its possibilities into the metaphorical garden of one's life?

Too often we forget to use what we already have. A friend of mine was trying to teach a small kitten that she had adopted how to play. So she got into her car, drove to a store, checked out various cat toys, waited in a long line, handed over too much money for several flimsy items, and drove back home. When she walked into her laundry room the kitten was playing with an old sock that had fallen behind the dryer.

When I worked as a developer of creative learning materials, I kept a small slip of paper pinned up on the bulletin board at eye level. On it were the words WHAT RESOURCES ARE AVAILABLE TO ME RIGHT NOW? That reminder saved me time and time again whenever "They-need-it-now" projects hit the desk.

Since then my priorities have shifted to suit a more natural rhythm of living. Yet I continue to try and look *right here* rather than *out there* for answers. If I forget, the combination of expended effort and the shortcomings of a more elaborate or costly solution conspire to remind me. Sooner or later, the very thing I was seeking quietly reveals its familiar if unacknowledged presence.

Almost everything I need for the garden I already have. Garlic cloves and onion skin, minced and mixed with water and a touch of vegetable oil, make a cheap and nontoxic bug deterrent. Many perennials can be divided and replanted, their seeds collected and shared. A leaky bucket may find new life as a container for mint. Shards of colorful dishes find new life, embedded in a homemade cement paving stone. A garden, mirroring nature, is the penultimate seedbed of creativity and resourcefulness.

But to recognize what I need, to distinguish it from what I think I want, requires quiet time and observation. We don't expect seeds to turn into fully formed flowers and vegetables

USING YOUR
ONION

❧

the moment they hit the soil. Yet how often do we expect solutions to blossom on demand? Then we grab at the first possible answer, not realizing that this early bloomer may turn out to be both fussy and short-lived. As my friend with the kitten learned, it's become almost reflexive in this culture to solve many common problems by literally shopping for their solutions. Phrases such as *make do, save up,* and *good as new* and words like *mend* and *refurbish* have all but disappeared from our vocabulary.

Yet the frugal gardener knows that one more fancy gadget or cute gardening hat could mean one less flowering shrub or several dozen fewer packets of seeds. Such a gardener learns to improvise and to find inherent abundance.

Where to learn this? From the garden, of course. When a poppy grows in a spot unsuited to the seeds it would normally let drop, it curls back its elongated seed pod and fires the seeds, as if from a cannon, toward more suitable ground. If that's not improvising, what is? As for abundance, the poppy seed epitomizes it. Each one is a speck no bigger than the average flea, yet each one holds in secret lush green leaves and lavish blooms.

The nineteenth-century English poet William Wordsworth charted the ways in which an increasingly technological, urbanizing, and consumerist culture endangers whatever is essentially and divinely human. Yet against a culture that, as Wordsworth predicted, threatened to dull the mind's "discriminatory powers" and "reduce it to a state of almost savage torpor," we can uphold and cherish the old, the natural, and even the thrown-away. Thus an old tire becomes a warming nest for heirloom tomatoes. The scrapings of the supper plate are composted into life-giving soil. An old blue glass insulator gathering dust in a junk drawer becomes a sun reflector among the marigolds.

Cultivate this attitude of cherishing and seeing into the ordinary. For it doesn't simply offer answers. It contains the entire Mystery. And that, paradoxically, is the ultimate answer to all our problems, questions, and confusions.

USING YOUR
ONION

Winter

TRUSTING

THE

FROST

The morning glory which blooms for an hour

Differs not at heart from the giant pine,

Which lives for a thousand years.

— Zen poem

IT'S ALL RENTED

At one point during my years in Ireland I lived in a small row-house that looked like a clone of all the other rowhouses on the street, but with one important distinction. Mine was rented.

To the solid-citizen homeowners, renters comprised a dubious underclass of flibbertigibbets and fly-by-nights. Regarded more as rovers than residents, our light attachment to land and property made us inherently suspect. That we might perch in a single spot for years on end carried no redemptive power; the invisible *R* each of us wore remained no less scarlet. Nor did a renter's mild-mannered ways fool anyone. The homeowners knew it was only a matter of time before the renter reverted to type and threw a party so wild it would shake the very cornerstones of civilization.

All right, not everyone thought that way. There were two young mothers in particular who became kind and helpful neighbors and whose children often called by for cups of tea and an exchange of storytelling. But there was also—well, I'll call him Mr. Fitz.

Poor Mr. Fitz. He was a hard-working man who came home right after work each evening, was infinitely kind and patient with his children, doted upon his missus and vice versa—and who never smiled. The cause of his misery? The source of his woe? The dark cloud on his otherwise bright horizon? Why, renters, of course.

As one of the banes of Mr. Fitz's existence, I did my best to alleviate his suffering by greeting him warmly whenever I strolled up the rented walkway to put a rented key into the rented door of the rented house that stood right next to his properly owned home, and in whose common wall molecules of both rented and mortgaged building materials mingled with lascivious abandon. Mr. Fitz's invariable response to my upstart salutations was to look at me like an injured dog being swabbed with vinegar. The nicer I was, the more his wariness increased. He knew I had to be up to something.

I was indeed. Behind each of the rowhouses ran long narrow plots that abutted a mirror-image row of neighboring plots and rowhouses. Although the constant rain-refreshened green of the grass was pleasant, only a few of the plots incorporated bona fide gardens—which seemed all the sadder in a country that features some of the most lavish gardens and amazing nature preserves in the Western world. (In a region known as the Burren, for example, Arctic and Mediterranean flowers grow side by side.)

So I jumped at the chance when friends who owned a home-based nursery offered me a few surplus flowers. The "few" plants turned out to be a truckload, with plenty to keep and plenty to share. When a delegation of the neighborhood children stopped by, we turned the yard work into an impromptu garden party. In those days, I knew nothing about soil amendment, couldn't tell an annual from a perennial, and probably enlisted several old kitchen utensils on a suicide mission as gardening tools. But somehow it all worked. The children made up their own names for the plants—Seamus's Pink Pinwheels, Fionnuala's Churchbell Flowers. To stay in the good graces of the landlady, we planted them along the margins of the lawn.

It wasn't long before Mr. Fitz got word of our pastoral high jinks. A long while he stood, arms folded, face inscrutable, leaning against the gray concrete wall that divided his orderly universe from the chaos I called home. He seemed desperate to make some kind of rational pronouncement. So I offered him some six-packs of flowers. To my lifelong delight, Mr. Fitz accepted them, and graciously too. Then, his face filled with sudden clarity as to what precisely had been troubling him about the whole mysterious procedure. He looked at me and said, "You're planting in rented soil! Why would you go to the bother of planting in rented soil?" He shook his head, thanked me again for the flowers, and walked away.

I will say, Mr. Fitz was more congenial to me after that. My apparent madness had provided me, as nothing else could, with a sole redeeming quality.

I've often thought about Mr. Fitz's pronouncement, the full if unintended implications of which were to change my life. For the truth is, it's *all* rented soil, every last inch and acre of the earth. Not a bit of it belongs to any one of us, although we may wave around private deeds, corporate contracts, and political treaties that claim otherwise. Instead it is we, as Chief Seattle and other wise elders knew, who belong to the land.

You may, for the time being, "have" anywhere from a quarter of an acre to a quarter of a million acres, but sooner or later the earth will welcome you back as a wandering child to her maternal embrace. Yet, far from reducing gardening to an exercise in futility, this raises it to the level of ritual.

Our work in the garden joins in the call-and-response of nature and human. We plant the seeds, nature sends the sun. We tend the blooms organically, nature sends birds, bees, and beneficial insects. We compost garden trimmings, and nature turns them back into nurturing soil. The blossom of one spring becomes the earth of another. So nature teaches us, along with many other lessons both delightful and severe, as we dance together to the music of time.

Our earthly lives themselves are on loan. Once, as I left a nursery carrying a flat of colorful perennials, I passed two women who were discussing which hair care products to purchase at the beauty supply next door. As I paused to readjust the heavily laden flat, one woman glanced at the miniature garden I carried and then remarked to her friend, "I can't see spending money on something that's just going to die." I suppressed the urge to tell her that her own money was about to be lavished on something that was already quite dead and that, alas, she herself, like all of us, would one day follow suit. Somehow I didn't think she'd thank me for the insight.

Yet that's the way it is. Life, as my mother used to say, is like a party. It starts before you arrive and keeps on going after you leave, so you might as well celebrate while you are here. *How* to celebrate, that's the question. Will you gobble up all the goodies for yourself, hoarding an experience that can never be owned? Or will you give a thought to those guests who are to come?

The most beautiful garden my maternal grandfather ever planted was one he knew he would never see. Aware that his cancer was terminal and his time was coming soon, Tom Collins went out one day and hid dozens and dozens of daffodil bulbs in his wife's flower beds. She had no idea he had done so until several weeks after his death, when the green leaves broke the ground. Then one day she stepped out on the back porch and there it was, a massy, golden surprise package, as potent as any love letter one could write.

There is a folk tale about an elderly man who plants a fruit tree. "Why are you going to all that trouble?" a little child asks him. "You know you won't live long enough to eat the fruit." "That does not matter," the old man replies. "When I was born there were fruit trees for me. Before I die, I need to plant fruit trees for others."

Clearly, we are called to stewardship, not ownership, of the earth, and for the gardener there are many ways to cultivate this relationship. Take the old man's story. We don't know where he planted the tree, only that somewhere a tree was needed. We, too, can plant trees in the larger garden of our local community, county, or beyond. The list that follows offers a few suggestions for getting started.

- *Host a garden party.* There are wedding showers and baby showers—why not garden showers? Help a nature-loving friend move into a new home by encouraging guests to bring gifts of seeds, plants, or other garden items. Or gather the troops and offer a day of weeding and digging so that your friend can jump ahead to more creative gardening.
- *If you live in an apartment complex, consider forming a container gardening group.* You can share tools and cut-

tings and buy products together to save money. Meet once or twice a month (rotating the venue among apartments) not only to exchange practical knowledge but to share accounts of gardens you have loved.

- *If you belong to a tenants' group, include the landscaping on your agenda.* In one apartment I lived in, a group of us convinced the manager to stop dousing the rosemary bushes with pesticide. As an herb, it is naturally resistant to insects. Besides which, we tenants wanted to inhale sweet fragrance, not toxic fumes.

- *Support — or help start — a community garden.* If you already have your "own" garden, you can still participate by sharing surplus gardening tools, plants and seeds, start-up labor, expertise, and other resources.

- *Apprentice yourself to one of nature's "master classes" by developing an ongoing relationship with the nearest wildlife area.* Make the preservation of this area a part of your gardening consciousness, whether by visiting regularly or donating funds or volunteer hours to a related organization.

- *Feed others as you feed yourself.* Donate surplus produce to a local food bank. Visit the website for Plant a Row for the Hungry (www.gwaa.org) and click the PAR icon to learn more about produce drop-off centers in your community.

- *Support a school gardening program or help get one started.* Proof that interest is growing came in 1999 when California Superintendent of Schools Delaine Eastin announced a "garden in every school" initiative that could lead to the greening of eight thousand public schools. The website for the National Garden Association (www.wowpages .com/nga) offers many links of interest to "growing minds."

- *Garden the nation.* Organizations like the American Community Gardening Association (www.communitygarden .org) and the National Arbor Day Foundation (www.arborday.org) have done much to bring nature back to the cities.

- *Turn prunings into possibilities.* Many towns and cities now organize annual giveaways of free cuttings, seeds, and plants donated by local gardeners. These events are also good places to pick up gardening wisdom and to find out more about the local environment. To find out more, contact a native plant society or other gardening club by checking the community listings of your local newspaper.

Wherever you live, think less in terms of what you own and more in terms of what can be sown. We each have the power to steward the earth, to nurture collective roots, and to share the harvest. And if, to paraphrase the wisdom of Mr. Fitz, our entire lives are an act of planting in rented soil, why not leave behind one heck of a garden?

Everything that grows holds perfection but a little moment.

— William Shakespeare

WHAT'S WRONG WITH THE PERFECT GARDEN?

Nothing kills a garden faster than perfectionism. It's the noxious weed that sends its roots deep into the most fertile soil there is, one's own psyche.

The effects of this toxic invader are subtle but vicious. Take this scenario. You're walking through your garden with a visitor. "What a beautiful garden!" your friend exclaims. No, it's terrible! you insist.

Your visitor, looking with fresh eyes, has taken in the garden as a whole. His or her garden vision is *organic,* and what could be more appropriate than that?

You, on the other hand, are trapped within the invisible underbrush of *Perfectus negativus.* Not only is your vision impaired, the weirdly twisted branches have a curious way of blocking out only the positive elements of the garden. Thus you fail to see the pincushion flowers spreading their pink and lavender carpets on either side of the jasmine-covered arbor— but you can spot at fifty paces the one petunia that needs deadheading. Your friend sees a cheerful crazy quilt of flowers; you see patches of dirt occasionally interrupted by chaos. Your friend sees the butterflies, goldfinches, and hummingbirds; you see the world's smallest snail. On and on it goes, until your perfectly pleasant garden becomes a jungle of defects.

Interestingly, the traditional Japanese garden, which seems to many people to center on an ideal of control, makes more room than Western gardens typically do for elements of imperfection. These elements include irregularity, perishability, and suggestion. According to such an aesthetic, the cherry tree whose tiny buds are barely visible, or whose branches are black and winter-bare, is graced with as much power to move the heart as a tree displaying its brief three days of snowy bloom.

The tree at its "imperfect" stages may even engage us in ways that the fully flowering tree does not. For the tree about to bloom excites hope, the skeletal tree in winter evokes memory, and both stages awaken our imaginations, opening rich stores of association and feeling as well as challenging us to cherish what is *as* it is. Would the pale blush pastels of a winter sky be as noticeable without the contrast of stark black branches?

The sunflowers in their full towering glory bring a smile to my face every summer, but it is the sight of the first shoots emerging from the soil, and of the faded dancers bowing their ragged heads, that strikes me to the heart.

Likewise, I'm beginning to feel more at peace with the rambling asymmetry of my ornamental garden. No matter how rigorously I tend it, the bare patches, extravagant outbursts, and demure groupings are always present, each state of being changing places with another, creating its own harmony of process.

In the imperfect garden, the beauty of the occasional bug-tattered blossom speaks of life. The spent tulips and daffodils allowed to fade so that their nutrients may feed the bulbs are a study in the magical powers of patience. The clipped hedge gone ragged again and the dandelion that springs up like a lighthouse overnight are nothing less than nature saying *Here I am!*

Fixation on achieving a perfect garden reduces the imaginative storehouse of innumerable visions down to one narrow picture. Like the virtual image that can never come out from behind the mirror, this rigidly defined garden can never take root in actual soil. When it governs your thinking, this very ideal becomes the black spot that blights your vision of the good-enough garden before you.

Allowed to spread, perfectionism can alter the very nature of your garden. Where once you tended energy, you find your-self performing drudgery. Energy gives back. Drudgery takes and keeps on taking.

So how do you nip this toxic crawler in the bud? Simple. Don't water it. Do expose it to plenty of sun. In other words, instead of wasting tears on what's less than idyllic in the gar-den, shine some clarity on everything that brings you joy. Then train that joy on some of the so-called flaws. Is that merely bare ground or a blank canvas you're looking at? Look at those spindly, dry poppy husks, some resembling unlit lanterns, others in the shape of furled umbrellas. Aren't they more beautiful for busying themselves with dropping the seeds of another summer's fiery carpet? Could that unweeded patch over there have something to do with the day that, catching a whiff of honeysuckle, lavender, and rose geranium, you wisely put down the trowel, set up the hammock, and allowed your-self to daydream?

My friend Sandra performs the following ritual at the end of every gardening day. As she sits and cleans her tools, she looks around the garden and takes inventory of everything that is going well. Sandra also recaps what she has just done and lets the sense of satisfaction sink in. This intention is made easier by the fact that she has allowed herself to enjoy each moment of *doing* every bit as much as the moment of *getting done.* What she does *not* do is look for flaws or use this state of happy tiredness to compile a mental list of further to-do's.

There will always be something to do in the garden, as in all of life.

❧

When I first began gardening, I tended to dissuade visitors from coming over. I wanted them to wait until my garden-in-progress was *done.* And of course it would never be done until it was perfect. Now I see that a garden—like a relationship, a home, a vocation, and a quest to learn—is *always* in progress.

And perfection isn't all it's cracked up to be.

Music, when soft voices die,

Vibrates in the memory;

Odours, when sweet violets sicken,

Live within the sense they quicken.

—Percy Bysshe Shelley

FLOWERS THAT LAST

Carnations have remarkable staying power.

So my father discovered once when he gave my mother two dozen garnet-red carnations for the usual reason—that is, no reason at all. My dad was like that. Which may help explain why they were still deeply in love more than forty years after their three-week courtship.

"I told the florist, 'Give me something that will last—just like my wife and me.'" My mother kissed him and set the carnations in a crystal vase to show off their pale green stems. Nearly two weeks later, the carnations looked as fresh as the day they came.

As an international airline pilot, Dad was away from his family for several days at a time. The upside to this was that he would then be home for several days at a time, a hands-on dad who changed diapers, hugged his sons as often as his daughters, and reveled in family life. When, after a flight to Rome and Cairo, Dad came home and saw the red carnations standing pertly in the vase, he nodded approvingly. "I told you they would last," he said proudly.

"Those carnations are really something," my mother agreed.

Another week, another flight. On his return, the carnations greeted my father like old friends. A week later when he set off to London, the carnations were still standing at attention as smartly as the guards at Buckingham Palace. Home he came and those carnations were still there, their stems somewhat shortened but otherwise looking no worse for wear. "Amazing," my father said.

Commenting on those amazing carnations soon became part of my father's routine. Their longevity was duly noted whenever he passed through the living room or set off for the other side of the world. Always when he returned, the carnations awaited him, more faithful than even the family dog (an unfortunate creature who was supposed to be a poodle but who looked more like a Brillo pad on legs).

One evening in early December, as my father was lighting logs in the stone fireplace, he and my mother chatted companionably. She had just come into the house with some fresh pine branches and was setting them into the vase to show off the carnations. My father looked over with satisfaction. "I told you those carnations would la—waaaiit a minute. Wait just one little minute."

"Yes?" my mother said sweetly.

I should probably explain at this point that my father, a keenly observant man out in the world, was nevertheless possessor of a trait very common, astrologically speaking, to home-loving Moon children. So relaxed would he feel, the moment he crossed our threshold, that he might not immediately notice that his wife had repainted the interior of the house in completely different colors, changed all the furniture in their bedroom, or turned the laundry room into a potting shed. Oh, he'd *feel* the difference, and he'd like it, but he'd just be so heck-sake at home with it that my mother usually had to point out what exactly the difference *was*. Had she removed the roof the better to view the stars, my father would have reveled in the constellations and only later commented that the room seemed more spacious somehow.

So there was my dad in December and it not-so-suddenly occurred to him that he had given "those carnations" to my mother back in—oh, say, June.

"Helen?" he said.

"Yes, Wally?" she replied. And they both burst out laughing.

"I thought you'd never notice," my mother said, indicating the synthetic stems of the fiendishly lifelike silk carnations. She'd come across them while he was on a flight about three weeks or so after the arrival of the genuine article. Waiting for Dad to notice the difference had become a kind of game, but she'd had no idea it was going to turn into a marathon.

Shortly after that, two dozen long-stemmed pink roses arrived at the door. You know, come to think of it, those roses sure lasted a long time. . . .

I tell this story so you know that I'm not thoroughly biased against artificial flowers. I'll grudgingly admit that they have their place, although I think that place is mainly in the realm of anecdote.

With that one exception, the cut flowers in our home were real. Every evening whichever child took his or her turn at setting the dinner table was also to take Mom's pruning shears and go out to the garden in search of blooms. Mixed into memories of homemade bouillabaisse and *spaghetti carbonara* on a school night are the heady scents of honeysuckle, roses, and a whole perfumery of geraniums. When it was my turn to help at the table, I set the forks beside the cloth napkins with all the speed of molasses running uphill in January. Then I threw myself into the flower gathering with a genuine passion, putting vases, both intended and improvised, at intervals along the table and all around the house.

It was my mother who told me the old Arabic saying, "If you have only two loaves of bread, sell one loaf to buy some roses." Even in winter, when fresh flowers were scarce, the hunt to find them became all the more important. Tiny but sturdy blooms came into their own, true to author Gertrude Wister's comment, "The flowers of late winter and early spring occupy places in our hearts well out of proportion to their sizes." To my mother's mind, no meal—not even peanut butter sandwiches around the kitchen table—was so plain, or any day so ordinary, that one could forgo the flowers. Better a wild daisy in a salt shaker than nothing, she would say. Otherwise you were just existing, not honoring the astounding fact of being alive.

The astounding or, at any rate, defining fact about artificial blooms is that they are *not* alive. It looks like a rose, a gladiolus, a chrysanthemum—but it isn't. Set it in a vase, stick it a room, live out the rest of your life, and, by golly, when they roll your carcass away that flower will still be there, same as it ever was. Just think. Robert Herrick would never have wept over daffodils that "haste away so soon." Instead, he might have assured us with the words, "Gather ye rosebuds whenever the heck you feel like it." Shakespeare, with no need to "consider everything that grows," might have had more time to tidy up his doublet drawer. Yes, there's a lot to be said for the practicality of artificial flowers.

It's just that a fake rose is a fake rose is a fake rose.

Take this simple test. Go into one of those humongous craft stores where several aisles are given over to fake flowers and watch what happens. Not much. Oh, the flowers sell, all right. People pick out what they want, toss it into the cart, and proceed to the fabric paint section. What's to keep them?

Then go to any establishment that offers real flowers for sale. It doesn't have to be an upscale florist's, either. One of my favorite places for fresh blooms is a little produce shop in Pacific Grove where inexpensive roses in every conceivable hue sit in buckets on either side of the door. Their scents are seductive enough to slow down even the crankiest Monday-morning warriors who attempt to pass them by. Some forgotten nerve endings start to wake and they find themselves lingering, trying to decide not which draft of the report should go to the department head but which roses look more like that morning's first rays, the pale gold or the blush pink. They may even, should the madness of real roses take full effect, begin *talking with other customers*. I've seen it happen to some of the stolidest citizens.

Once, I went to a party where the hosts had set artificial flowers around the house in clear glass vases partially filled with water. A clever touch, that. It made you wonder and draw near. However, once people had figured it out, their interest quickly shifted elsewhere. Far from lasting, the fake flowers suddenly ceased to exist for them at all. Those few people who did linger invariably commented that they would never have known the flowers were fake. Then the conversation would turn to the cost of things, stores, how things were going at work, how busy everyone was, and so on.

But you set fresh flowers in a vase and people's oh-so-hungry senses kick in and cook up a feast of associations. The connection between the olfactory sense and memory has long been established. A whiff of lilacs, the touch of a tender petal, and someone recalls that the covered terrace at their grandparents' old house was draped in lilac. Which reminds them of this great story, a story that, with the sensory magic of the flowers, triggers others' experiences, too.

You want sound bites? Stick with fake. But bring nature into the circle and, like real flowers warmed by the sun, the immense garden of language will come into sudden bloom.

What wondrous life is this I lead!

Ripe apples drop about my head;

The luscious clusters of the vine

Upon my mouth do crush their wine;

The nectarine and curious peach

Into my hands themselves do reach;

Stumbling on melons, as I pass,

Ensnared with flowers, I fall on grass.

—Andrew Marvell,
"Thoughts in a Garden"

THE WORLD'S HAPPIEST GARDENERS

One of my favorite gardening books is a faded treasure I found in a secondhand shop. Published in 1959 by Rodale Books, *The World's Happiest Gardeners* features first-person essays by one upbeat toiler after another. "Our Garden Saved Us $10 a Week!" cheers one family. "Our most prized possession is our compost pile!" cries another. A nine-year-old child rhapsodizes, "Oh, Mother, don't you just *love* earthworms?"

There's not a curmudgeon in sight, and if these cheery souls have ever felt discouraged, they guard that information more carefully than the secret of growing Lazy Man's Roses or raising Giant Crops on a Midget Homestead.

The high queen of *The World's Happiest Gardeners* is surely Ruth Stout, who even then was celebrated for her unorthodox methods, sense of humor, and indefatigable belief in the potential of a seed. "Summer usually begins full of promise," she writes, "and in spite of years of experience I see, in looking forward, fine roses, gorgeous annuals, large Blue Hubbard squash, perfect heads of cabbage, wonderful corn, bright orange pumpkins, onions big enough to astonish people. I forget about black leaf spot, squash borers, cabbage worms, drought, the whole long list of character-builders. I get plenty of setbacks, but whatever disaster one day may bring, you feel sure, if you were born an optimist, that tomorrow has some nice surprise for you."

As if to underscore this optimism, Stout mentions that she is sharing these rosy sentiments not in a time of lush flowering or abundant harvest but on a cold, windy day in March, "when snowstorms and blizzards are still possible and high winds a safe bet."

Yet Stout was mistaken about one thing. Back in 1959, having "gone beyond three score and ten," she declared herself to be in the evening of her life. In fact, Stout had barely crossed the threshold of her life's afternoon. She continued to garden well into her late nineties, passing away in 1984. Could this longevity have had anything to do with believing that to-morrow, like some mysterious seed, holds within it the possibility of verdant surprise? How could it not?

On the cover of *The World's Happiest Gardeners* is a smiling young Nancy Drew look-alike in sleeveless Peter Pan shirt and sky-blue Bermuda shorts. She holds out a basket, or perhaps an upturned sun hat, filled with Kodachrome-tinted flowers. Her obvious joy in gardening is undiminished by the fact that she is wearing a pair of high heels.

In white, no less.

Far from triggering my cynicism, that silly but earnest image has become a kind of holy card to me. I look at it on days when the only green thing in the garden is my envy of other, more glorious gardens. Then I exhort my inner farmer. "Look, if Nancy Drew can create an organic haven in little white pumps, then—by golly!—you can put on your sweats and sneakers and go turn the compost." If you wish to try this at home, do remember that "by golly!" is an important part of the mantra.

Gardeners are an optimistic lot.

This is not to say that each and every gardener is a paragon of good cheer. A gardener may wear a glower like Beethoven's more often than the smile of Pollyanna. He or she may be less inclined to frolic than to fret among the wildflowers. Still, that gardener is an optimist. For who but an optimist buries an unpromising object the size of a teardrop in the ground and believes that months later it will emerge as the very definition of beauty, sustenance, or both?

Sometimes it does, often it doesn't. But no gardener worth her—uh, silt would dream of giving up. Oh, she might weep, scowl, kick something inanimate (plastic pots do nicely), even coin colorful new expressions on the spot—but never give up. To a gardener, there's no such thing as a lost cause, only the promise of next spring.

Among the plants I have cultivated most avidly is one I have never succeeded in harvesting. Not *yet*. The first time I attempted eggplant, I made the fatal mistake of purchasing drugstore specials. With their glossy dark leaves they looked invincible—until I got them into the ground, whereupon they folded up like dead bats. At the time, it seemed as if the obvious solution was to douse the miserable specimens in commercial fertilizer. The result? *Giant* miserable specimens, which not even the gophers would eat. That was the year I decided to find out about organic gardening.

The following spring, fired up by a new enthusiasm for organics and wishing to practice frugality, I attempted to grow eggplants from seed. The process kept me as busy as a nurse in a preemie ward, but the transplants I fussed over so mightily collapsed upon entry into the world outdoors. That was the year I decided to learn about such things as weather awareness, hardening off, and side-dressing.

Another spring, another try. I opted for organic seedlings, which thrived—until they were overshadowed by towering tomato plants. An attempted transplant failed, and although I planted new seedlings in a more suitable spot, the weather had begun to cool just when the budding globes were most in need of heat.

Why, then, am I so happy about my nonexistent crop? Because I'm getting closer! Every failure has taught me something, so that every season I go about the process a little better informed. Even that genius Thomas Edison experienced thousands of "failures" on the way to developing the lightbulb. If he could handle it, I can persist in cultivating eggplant. This summer, it's harvest home for sure.

As a gardener, all my todays are the seeds of tomorrow's bloom. Hard weather today merely assures me that better weather is coming. Tomatoes that wilt on the vine give rise to visions—albeit teary-eyed visions—of next summer's gravid champions. And while I'm thrilled if you admire my daffodils in the spring, they never looked more dazzling to me than on the cold, gray day I raked away stones, worked my spade and fingernails into the dirt, and planted the knobbly brown bulbs.

The connection between gardening and optimism has not gone unnoticed by the medical world, which has sought to formalize that natural liaison in a process known in clinical circles as "horticultural therapy." According to several sources, a primary benefit of horticultural therapy is that it places the client in a safe nonthreatening environment. Other alleged benefits include improved ability to express one's feelings and increased feelings of being in control.

Now wait just one Freudian minute. Are we talking about *gardening*? Or are we talking about a practice that can include hard labor, stinging nettles, sharp thorns, pebbles in the shoe, mud up to the elbows, manure all over the place, disease, pestilence, bad weather, a dozen wasps to every butterfly, and a guarantee of occasional failure? You call *that* safe and nonthreatening? As for expressing one's feelings, that much is certainly true, for I have previously alluded to the vigorous and colloquial ways in which gardening has led me to explode with—or, rather, express—my own feelings, but perhaps that is not what the psychologists have in mind.

That leaves the notion that gardening increases one's sense of being in control. In *control*? Personally, I have never felt less in control than when I consigned a tiny seed to the vagaries of nature, waited for warm weather to break through the cloud cover and bless the tomatoes, or wondered why a neglected volunteer survived where pampered plantings shriveled up and died. If that's control, I'd sure hate to experience helplessness.

No, I think the psychologists have once again gotten it wrong. Finding safety, getting into socially acceptable touch with appropriate feelings, and being in control—it all sounds nice, but I suspect that even if any of it were true, it would still have nothing to do with the reason for gardening's overwhelming popularity.

Ultimately, I think, gardening speaks to a deep-seated (deep-seeded?) desire to experience the real, the essential, the astonishingly possible. To garden is gradually to give up control, to fall literally to one's knees and come into closer and closer contact with the tremendous and often bewildering beauty of the living world. Nothing, you find, is at all what you thought it was. Dirt is not dirt, but a teeming mass of microorganisms that turn death back into life. A tree is not just a tree but a far-reaching, history-holding, and life-sustaining place, the grand entry to which may be smaller than a grain of sand. Weather, you come to realize, is not a five-minute report on TV but the earth having its say—the least attended yet the truest voice amid our increasingly high-tech shouting match.

Your entire outlook can shift like a haphazardly tossed bulb righting its position in the earth, the better to break through and flower. Growing down becomes as important as growing up. Trusting the frost in winter brings you the peach in summer. Witnessing all that can struggle, flourish, and heal, given a bit of earth, you experience your own inclusion, and amazement blossoms into gratitude.

To those who have not yet learned the secret of true happiness, begin now to study the little things in your own dooryard.

—George Washington Carver:
In His Own Words

AFTERWORD

Not long after my mother's death, I was turning the soil in what had only days before been a grassy area. Ripping out the chemical-greedy lawn to make way for native plants had seemed like a good idea at first, but now, as I stood surveying what seemed like an endless plain of dirt, I felt thoroughly daunted. What did I know about gardening? Not a thing. Discouraged, I dropped the shovel and decided to check the mail instead. Anything to get away from contemplating the impossible.

The one person who could have advised me on how to get started was gone. Brooding, I trudged up the hill to the mailbox. There then occurred the kind of event that comes to everyone who has ever lost a loved one, the kind of moment when the phone rings or someone knocks at the door and you are pierced through with the sudden realization of who it will *not* be. For it struck me that I was, out of habit, checking the mail to see if there was a letter from Mom. And of course there would not be. Never would be again.

Stung by the absoluteness of death, I continued to walk up the hill. The heavy spring rains had coaxed wild grasses as fine as baby's hair out of the soil where the chaparral ran up to either side of the driveway. The odor of sage, its still-glistening leaves beginning to warm under the sun, wafted through the air. Stopping to pluck and bruise a leaf of it between my fingers, I nearly tripped over a family of quail that darted across the drive, six fluffy, rambling chicks, with a nervous parent at either end attempting to keep them in line. In my surprise, I slipped unceremoniously onto my bottom and startled what seemed like hundreds of tiny junco finches into sudden flight above the thick undergrowth of manzanita, sage, yarrow, and coyote bush.

I stood up and looked at the scene. The sloping hillside was punctuated by great oak trees. I have been around oak trees since I first climbed up into the great arms of one at age five, but it wasn't until that day that I noticed something surprising about them, something perhaps very ordinary to those of you who have known about it all along. *The oak trees had broken into flower.*

Oh, they were tiny beyond belief and the palest of greens, yet they were not leaves but very much flowers in their own right. How could I have lived so long and not noticed this before?

Lizards, rabbits, and blue jays skittered among the underbrush, where hidden purple irises blossomed as if for their own amusement. The air sang, not only with jays, finches, hummingbirds, and hawks but with saffron dragonflies, night-and-day striped bumblebees, and barely discernible clouds of lesser wings. Not even the asphalt driveway was barren. Ants swarmed along the edges, and here and there an obsidian beetle or a sow bug the color of lapis lazuli could be seen. Coast prettyface and other wildflowers turned the tiniest cracks in the asphalt into gardens. It was death, not life, that was the fragile one. Everywhere I looked, life was asserting itself. No fallen leaf, no heavy stone, no wounded creature's discarded shell could hold it back. Life was persistent, trumpeting its presence again and again and again.

In the mailbox there were the usual bills and a flyer advertising a new cable service. I carried them down the hill, feeling strangely better than when I had walked up. As I was about to drop the flyer into the recycle bin, something caught my eye, something that moved across the paper. Smaller than a question mark, little more than an emerald green speck, it moved with determination to complete its all-important eight-inch journey. I guided it toward a leaf of the wisteria. At least I think I did. It was so small there was no way to know. Nor had I the least clue what it might be. I only knew it was alive. Hugely and undeniably alive.

AFTERWORD

A memory came to me then, or rather, a powerful moment drew me back into its presence. My mother is at home in bed. She is in the last stages of cancer. Yet whenever new nurses come by they are visibly struck by her extraordinary beauty, as if all that was joyful in her has been distilled into the translucence of her face. Now she speaks to my brother Michael, my sister-in-law Bernice, and me. Later, people will tell us that she was simply hallucinating, speaking nonsense, reacting to painkillers. We know better. What Mom does is to gesture at the space between us. "Isn't that interesting," she says. "Do you see it? It's a green thread, like a law, and it connects us all."

The poet William Blake, who also had visions, spoke of a golden thread, which, if followed, would lead one back to the Holy City of Jerusalem. I have seen, and felt the texture of, my mother's green thread, and I will follow it from garden to garden, wherever it goes.

The following spring, with the plain of dirt beginning to transform itself into a garden, I took cuttings from the rosemary. This, you may recall, is the plant that had started it all, the signifier of remembrance, whose significance I had not even guessed at when I carried it from my mother's garden to my own. Now the parent plant was thriving and it was time to gather cuttings for new young shoots. They would not react well at first, drooping for a while like ones who have lost hope. Then, finding their own roots, and setting those roots deeper and deeper into the earth where all that seems to be separate is reunited, they would take heart. And grow.

RECOMMENDED READING

Borland, Hal. *Sundial of the Seasons*. Philadelphia: J. B. Lippincott Co., 1964. This out-of-print book is well worth searching for at your library or favorite used bookshop.

Fleischman, Paul. *Weslandia*. Cambridge, Mass.: Candlewick Press, 1999. Have a packet of jumbo seeds ready to plant the minute you finish reading this whimsical tale to your favorite young people.

Madison, Deborah, and Edward Espe Brown. *The Greens Cookbook: Extraordinary Vegetarian Cuisine from the Celebrated Restaurant*. New York: Bantam Books, 1987. This delightful compendium will tell everything you want to know about cooking the greens that you grow.

Meehan, Maude. *Washing the Stones: The Collected Poetry of Maude Meehan*. Watsonville, Calif.: Papier Mache Press, 1996. Meehan's lyric poems, with their themes of nature, the cycle of life, and human rights, have won over even those who claim to dislike poetry.

Murray, Elizabeth. *Cultivating Sacred Space: Gardening for the Soul.* Rohnert Park, Calif.: Pomegranate, 1998. In poetic photographs and text, Murray invites you into a garden of serenity and guides you in creating one of your own.

Murray, Elizabeth. *Monet's Passion: Ideas, Inspiration, and Insights from the Painter's Garden.* Petaluma, Calif.: Pomegranate Press, 1989. While gardening books on this scale often intimidate the average gardener, this one will release your inner artist.

Nabhan, Gary Paul, and Stephen Trimble. *The Geography of Childhood: Why Children Need Wild Places.* Boston: Beacon Press, 1995. This is an eye-opening and moving examination of children's need for daily relationship with nature.

Riotte, Louise. *Carrots Love Tomatoes: Secrets of Companion Planting for Successful Gardening.* Pownal, Me.: Storey Books, 1998. This is the definitive guide to matchmaking your plants.

Stewart, Sarah. *The Gardener.* New York: Farrar, Straus & Giroux, 1998. In this utterly engaging story, a young girl creates an unforgettable urban garden.

ABOUT THE AUTHOR

JOYCE MCGREEVY is a writer of creative nonfiction and a longtime gardener. A regular contributor of home and garden articles to the *Monterey County Herald,* she has also written a children's book and was the publicist for the Western Stage, a nationally recognized theater company in Salinas, California. McGreevy graduated with honors in English and Philosophy from the University of Ireland, Galway, where she lived for several years and where she received awards for both journalism and poetry. She lives in Monterey County, California.